"Mark's book provides a roadmap for living a happy and healthy life as we age, and it is filled with practical advice and inspiring stories. I am particularly impressed with Mark's emphasis on the importance of seeing the world through different lenses. As we age, it is important to remain open-minded and curious, and to challenge our own biases and prejudices. This can help us to live more fulfilling lives and to connect with people from all walks of life. I believe that Mark's book is a valuable resource for anyone who wants to age gracefully. It is a book that will stay with you long after you finish reading it."

—Pete Danielson, VP marketing development, Service Nation

"Similar to his other books, we meet another one of Mark's amazing mentors, William. He is wise, funny, and loves to share his knowledge and life experiences ... the perfect mentor. As in all of Mark's books there is a never-ending push towards positivity, backed up with a range of wise quotes from great leaders, such as Marcus Aurelius, who is the main source of quotes on living and altitude in this book. This book helps people to understand why rock stars live so long ... they love what they do and never retire, hence they seem ageless. The lessons shared on being excessively young will resonate with readers of all ages."

—David Francis, ICT tracker

"Mark has done it again. Like so many of his other works, I will be acquiring multiple copies of this one to share with coworkers, friends, family, and anyone who is in my circle of influence. It's a guidebook for living better. I will be reading this one again and again as a reference. Thanks so much, Mark, for sending me this copy. Once I started reading it, I literally finished it over two days (That's quick for me)."

—Steven Long, residential division president, GSM Services

"Mark always delivers insightful wisdom in a digestible format. His writing and mentorship helped me begin a growth transformation journey many years ago. This book reminds me of a passage by Elie Wiesel in his book Souls on Fire: *When you die and meet your maker, all you will be asked is, 'Why didn't you become you? Why didn't you become all that you are?'* Mark provides actionable guidance to help us pursue our Ikigai. I know you will enjoy his latest book."

—Ryan Kalmbach, visionary, Johnstone Supply, the Orion Group

"For many years now I have been one of the lucky ones with a front-row seat to watch Mark's trek toward being 'old.' Unlike most of us, he's watched and learned every step of the way. This book bundles all that wisdom and grace into a fun, interesting, and rewarding journey. I've read them all, and I think this is Mark's best yet."

—Andy Armstrong, author, *The Grace Arsenal*

"Mark symbolizes the definition of effective leadership. He has truly mastered the art of being succinct, profound, and life-changing, all within a few words. For anyone stuck, lost, or looking for a next chapter in life, Mark's books serve as the mentor you never knew you had. When I'm Old captures some of Mark's best life lessons in an easy-to-read format that anyone can learn from at any age. It will teach you how to live longer, love stronger, and cherish more of your life."

—Randall Chenworth, director of education, MCA

"Mark is my Ferris Bueller. He taught me that life moves pretty fast and you better stop and look around. You know what I like about Mark? Everything! Mark is a rising tide. He lifts everyone. Mark's latest book will lift you up. Enjoy …"

—Kevin Thomas, entrepreneur

When I'm Old

ALSO BY MARK MATTESON

Freedom From Fear
Freedom From Fear Forever
A Simple Choice
It's About TIME
Freedom From FAT
Old Light Through New Windows
As We THINK So We BECOME

EBOOKS

Wag More, Bark Less
Sales Success Stories
Customer Service Excellence
Presenting Like a Pro
You Don't Have to Be Sick to Get Better
Sparking Sales Success (How to Enjoy a 75% Close Ratio)

When I'm Old

Mark Matteson

Ugly Dog Publishing

Dedication

*To my good friend, Jason Liller, for your hard work
turning my stories into finished books.
Thank you for making me look better than I am!*

Published by **Ugly Dog Publishing,** Edmonds, WA

ISBN 978-0-9995350-6-6

Designed and printed in the United States of America

Contents

Foreword by Luther Clemons

I am past the three-quarter mark on my life's journey and gratefully continue to travel that path that all of us are on. Mark Matteson is one person I am proud that I did not miss on the way. Many years ago, I met Mark at a business meeting where he was the keynote speaker. His communication style concerning business, platform skills, and life lessons in general grabbed and kept my attention.

We continue to stay in touch, and I consider him a friend. I have hired him multiple times for speaking engagements at my company's business meetings and he always makes it entertaining, memorable, and worth every penny.

After reading Mark's previous books, I can truthfully say I consider *When I'm Old* to be his best work. This little fable guides you through deeper choices in life's journey and gives you a range of insights to help you find your own understanding and meaning in life.

Mark, I know you are a big basketball fan, so I want to say, you have a triple-double here!

Luther Clemons, COO and chairman of the board,
Associated Equipment

Introduction

His name was William Ian Oldham. I was listening to him read his book, *Sages, Stoics, and Poets* in rush-hour traffic. I pulled over to write a quote in my journal from Marcus Aurelius that he repeated twice for emphasis. I've never forgotten it: *"It is not death that a man should fear, but he should fear never beginning to live!"*

Of all the Stoics, William quoted Marcus Aurelius most often. His recall was extraordinary and always at just the right time in my life.

Many historians claim Marcus was the finest emperor in Rome's extraordinary history. His book, *Meditations,* was never meant for public consumption, but Willam's book ended every chapter with a quote from Marcus. It wasn't just the cogent content of Mr. Oldham's book that made it striking, it was also his delivery, eloquent and inspiring. His voice, think Anthony Hopkins doing Shakespeare, transformed his words into earth-shaking insights. I had to meet this man, this author, this thespian. I called the number in the back of the book. His secretary answered and informed me he was traveling on a twenty-city book tour but assured me she would forward my message. He called me the next day. I agreed to come to the reading, as it just so happened he was speaking that night at Elliott Bay Books in downtown Seattle, the most famous bookstore in the state. Two hours before he was to conduct his reading, we met for tea.

3

He came down the stairs of the W Hotel, his elegant fedora tipped rakishly to the left. He was tall and lean in his three-piece suit, shoes shined like a mirror, with a blue bow tie and matching handkerchief in his pocket. His cane was magnificent, with an elephant's head (When I asked him, "Why an Elephant?" he replied, "My dear boy, the elephant never forgets!").

He smiled when he saw me approach. "What an absolute pleasure to meet you, young man. Let's have some tea," he said with an air of both confidence and humility.

He was 65 years young but he looked 45; his aspect confident but warm, vigorous yet compassionate, intense yet sincere. He would go on to live a good long life, 95 years to be exact, ever investing his time helping others to release their potential and achieve their goals. He would quite simply change my life. Of course, I wouldn't know that then. How could I? He was just an Englishman in Seattle.

I learned that his parents were English and that his father had fought in World War II. "My mother was born in England in 1932," I said, in an effort to make a connection. "Her father was killed in that same war. She told me more than once that she missed him terribly. She treasured the old black-and-white pictures of this tall, handsome, regal fellow. She claimed that I had my grandfather's nose." William listened patiently and smiled. He went on to tell me that his mother, too, loved the military and often told stories of famous English military heroes. In fact, he was named after William the Conqueror. William's knowledge and recall of history was extraordinary and detailed.

William's middle name was Ian (the Scottish name for John, meaning *God is gracious*). I like that. "A man's name should mean something," he said to me one day. In truth, he was most probably named after the novelist Ian Fleming, who wrote the James Bond novels. He loved those books. He had them on a special shelf in his library, every one of them, beginning with *Casino Royale*.

4

Oldham is a surname meaning *old lands* with origins tracing to the town of Oldham in Greater Manchester, England.

There you have it. A Norman invader, a gracious bestselling author from an old land. All this over tea to a fan he had only just met a short time before.

He would write handwritten thank-you notes, include a clever couplet at the end of each one, and always sign his name in upper caps W.I.O. which he used to say meant *When I'm Old*, as in, "When I'm Old I will retire and do what I really love." This was ironic as it was clear he WAS doing what he loved. I could sum up his personality with one word: PASSION!

When asked, "How are you today, William?" he often replied in one of five ways: *"Good as gold, Right as rain, Cool as a cucumber, Sound as a pound,* and *Fit as a fiddle!"* or some combination of those alliterations. The thing is, he meant it. And—he *was.*

More often than not, as he would listen, he would say, "Indeed" and would end a conversation with a promise like, "It's a deal!"

After his funeral, I talked with those who knew him best. Like an ace reporter, I asked his friends and family every question I could think of to get to know him better. Why? I owed him a debt I could never repay. Whenever I thanked him for helping me solve a problem, he would say the same thing: "Don't tell anyone I helped, and try to help at least two other people like I helped you. Give it away to keep it, young man!" That was William: philosopher, coach, mentor, teacher.

What follows are the things I learned from my mentor, William Ian Oldham. I will spend the rest of my life trying to fill his enormous size-14 shoes. I miss him every day.

1

On Aging

The days go by so fast now, as I turn the calendar pages,
Another year behind me, as my face slowly ages.

Now that I am 65 years young, I have reached that time in a person's life when they are sent out to pasture because of a calendar date. Not me. I am rethinking my position. In fact, I have "No desire to retire!" I am simply asking myself in every situation, *What would William do or say?* I believe he lived to be 95 years young because he never stopped doing what he loved most: helping others. He did what he loved, he loved what he did. He admired Mose Allison, the jazz icon, often quoting one of his songs: *"I love the life I lead and lead the life I love!"*

I have been learning that if you do what you love, you will never work another day in your life. It's passion and preference. That distinction can change your life, your perspective, and give meaning and purpose to all you do—which ultimately adds years to your life and life to your years.

I have a childhood friend who works in a job he hates and has done so for over 45 years. He is one of the unhappiest people I know. He has lots of toys but no joys. It's sad, really.

In the early eighties I was fixing an ice machine in Seattle at the Horizon House, a very upscale, high-end senior community. The lunch bell rang and 35 women were chasing one guy, George. He was 88 years young. The most popular guy in the building. The thought occurred to me, *If a man lives long enough, the women chase him!* I was 25. Over the next year a single question kept pecking at me like the raven in Edgar Allen Poe's poem: *What happened to all the dudes? How come 35 women and only one George?* I began reading everything I could find on longevity, which led me to one uncommon conclusion: *If you do what you love, you will never work another day in your life!* It turns out that people who follow their bliss, who love their work, who see it as play, whether they work for someone else or are self-employed, are not only happier and more fulfilled, they earn more money and live considerably longer lives than those who see their job as drudgery, and they have a better time along the way.

William used to say, "I GET to do this ... there are no HAVE TO's in my life."

In Japan, the concept is called *ikigai.* Ikigai is simple, not easy. Ikigai means *life purpose* or *raison d'être.* It refers to defining your personal meaning of life in relation to your talents, passions, and profession, as well as what you can give to the wider world for a lifetime. Ikigai asks several questions:

1. What do I love doing?
2. What am I passionate about?
3. What am I really good at?
4. What does the world need?
5. What is my mission?

6. What is my true calling?
7. What is the world willing to pay for?

And so, the journey of discovery and enlightenment began. As I began to research longevity, a common thread began to emerge from men who retired. *If I am what I do, when I don't I am not!* What? If you are your job, when you retire—now you are less than? Evidently. For 68% of American *men* in this country, that sad fact is true, according to two separate studies by IBM and Xerox. Two out of three men who retire in this country are dead within 18-24 months of retirement. Shocking but avoidable.

So why do these men die so young? My theory consists of four simple reasons:

1. They don't *exercise* on a daily basis. (Obesity kills.)
2. They don't *eat properly* or in smaller portions. (You are what you eat.)
3. They don't *communicate* about real stuff, keeping it all inside. (Silence isn't golden; it's deadly!)
4. They retire to *nothing*. (There's no meaning or purpose in their lives, no ikigai.)

It's my firm belief that women never really retire. They find meaning, purpose, and balance from motherhood, grandmotherhood, community, and friends. Is it any wonder women live longer than men? It seems to me women's worth comes from different places than men's—family, friends, and community. For men, our work is worth and worth our work.

I was 32 years old when my light came on. William suggested I listen to Earl Nightingale's audio program, *Lead the Field*. It changed my direction and my life. I didn't know how I was going to earn a living as a writer and speaker, but I knew I would figure it out. Ten years later I was doing both full-time. William inspired me to follow in his footsteps.

George Burns, the iconic actor, singer, comedian, and author who lived to be 99 said, *"I would rather be a failure at something I love than a success at something I hate."*

George Bernard Shaw, the playwright, author, and critic, at age 92, wrote, *"The people who get on in this world are the people who get up and look for the circumstances they want, and if they can't find them, make them!"*

Armand Hammer, the great industrialist, at 92 said, *"I love my work. I can't wait to start a new day. I never wake up without being full of ideas. Everything is a glorious challenge."*

So it's about finding and following your *Bliss?* Webster defines Bliss as *Complete Happiness, Heaven, Paradise. Spiritual Joy, Ecstasy.*

Do What You Love

Find and follow your bliss. After years of searching I discovered that my bliss is speaking, writing, podcasting, coaching, and helping others achieve their goals. William challenged me to read two books a week. I took it to heart. Over the last 30 years I have read over 3,000 books. From that research, certain questions emerged:

1. *If every job paid a dollar, which job would you do?*
2. *What did you LOVE to do at age seven? (Ask your mum.)*
3. *What specific activity do you engage in that causes time to stand still because you are lost in the joy of the activity?*
4. *If a doctor told you that you had six months to live, how would you spend your time?*
5. *If you inherited $10,000,000, what would you do differently?*

Once you answer these questions honestly and thoroughly, simply ask yourself, *What are the common denominators? What are the threads that connect the answers?* The answer to THOSE questions is your bliss.

Shakespeare wrote in *Hamlet,* *"To thine own self be true."*

Most people live their whole lives and never surrender to that simple truth.

When you find the common thread to all five questions, THAT is your bliss, your ikigai. Follow your bliss and the money will follow, with one disclaimer: First, invest seven years or 10,000 hours of hard work and study, whichever comes first. I tell this to high school and college athletes when I speak to them. Finding a career based on bliss is very different than a job or a career; it's really a calling. Sadly, only 5% of the population ever really surrenders to a calling they believe in.

These days, my play is work, my work play. When I am reading the *New York Times,* watching a movie, reading a biography, attending a concert, listening to music, attending a basketball game, or working out at the club, it's all work ... and play. I am looking for the causes of success, the clues, the habits of successful people. It's all connected, blurred in a wonderful kind of jambalaya of joy!

Much to my wife's consternation, I want to be George from the senior community, alive at 95 like William Ian Oldham! I want to be the last man standing. How about you?

We must welcome the future, remembering that soon it will be the past; and we must respect the past, remembering that it was once all that was humanly possible.

When you arise in the morning, think of what a precious privilege it is to be alive—to breathe, to think, to enjoy, to love.
Marcus Aurelius

2

On Getting Old Is Not for Wimps

Getting old is not for wimps, I heard my father say,
Yet I'm as old as he once was, that time is today.

My father was a big strong guy, 6'4" and 225 pounds of muscle. He was all-state in three sports—baseball, basketball, football—and he was a six handicap in golf! He pitched in the major leagues, played football in college, and semipro basketball in Germany. He walked every day, did push-ups, sit-ups, and stretching every night, religiously, until Alzheimer's changed his routines and habits. He used to say, "Getting old is not for wimps!" Except the term he actually used was *namby-pamby*. Being such an old expression, I looked it up: "wimp, crybaby, coward, WEAKLING. You never hear namby-pamby today. Pity. The opposite of namby-pamby is strength, courage, taking risks, persistence, stretching comfort zones, and living life to the fullest.

Now that I am the same age he was when I first heard that, I believe the point he was making is that getting old is often painful. Things change. You begin to have pain like arthritis, sore back and knees, achy joints, and so on. Suck it up. You are on this side of the grass, not pushing up daisies. Be grateful for life's many blessings that only age and experience brings, like:

- Grandchildren
- Wisdom
- Resources
- Lifelong Relationships
- Opportunity
- Knowledge
- Productivity
- Effectiveness
- Gratitude
- Wonder
- Life lines (some call them wrinkles)
- Appreciation of nature
- Not caring what other people think

Clint Eastwood said, *"Aging can be fun if you lay back and enjoy it!"*

Drew Barrymore said, *"From my perspective, there is no reason to be afraid of aging, because if you age, you're lucky! The alternative is death."*

William pulled a great story out of his hat one day over tea. "One of my favorite stories about General U.S. Grant and President Abe Lincoln goes like this [I am paraphrasing]—"The tide had finally turned for the North during the Civil War. An exhausted Lincoln had finally found a general who would fight and win battles. He had gone through one hapless leader after another until he found the right guy. Grant knew how to do one thing: charge. He fought. General Sherman complained to Lincoln that the rumor from the front was that Grant was a drunk, drinking whiskey and smoking cigars each night. "Really?" Lincoln said. "Well then, find out what kind of whiskey he drinks and cigars he smokes and give them to all the other generals!"

Sipping his tea as if to prepare himself for the next act in a play, he continued. "Grant's reputation has fallen into disrepair. Many Americans view him as a caricature: someone 'uniquely stupid,' an insensitive butcher as a general, an incompetent mediocrity as president, and a drunk. Several efforts to counter this stereotype have often gone too far in the other direction, resulting in an equally distorted laudatory portrait of near perfection. In reading the original sources, many historians are convinced that Grant was neither a bumbling idiot who was the darling of fortune, nor a flawless general who could do no wrong. Rather, he was a tangle of opposing qualities—a relentless warrior but a generous victor, a commander who drew upon uncommon sense in drafting campaign plans and in winning battles, a soldier so sensitive to suffering that he could not stand to see the bloody hides at his father's tannery, a man who made mistakes and sometimes learned from them. Even as he waged war, he realized the broader political implications of the struggle; he came to believe that the preservation of the Union depended upon the destruction of slavery. Equally compelling is Grant's personal story—one of a man who struggled against great odds, bad luck, and personal humiliation, who sought joy and love in the arms of his wife and his children, and who was determined to overcome adversity and prevail over his detractors. 'None of our public men have a story so strange as this,' William T. Sherman remarked, noting that Grant remained a mystery even to himself."

It's safe to say Grant was not a wimp or a namby-pamby.

15

Getting old is a privilege and an honor. As Louis Armstrong sang in the song by George David Weiss and Bob Thiele, *I think to myself, What a wonderful world.*

Let's take a page from General Grant's book and charge!

You have power over your mind—not outside events. Realize this, and you will find strength.
Marcus Aurelius

3

On Complaining and Criticizing

But when I'm old, much older than this day,
I'll keep my griping to myself, complaining doesn't pay.

Why do we complain and criticize? It's one my most challenging defects of character that I have spent the better part of my adult life working to eliminate. So why is it so hard to do? When I asked William, he said, "Why do people complain and criticize? I have a few theories:

It's easy to do
It quickly becomes a bad habit
Most people do it, it's the rule, not the exception
I feel a kind of moral superiority when I engage in it
It's a low self-esteem issue
To get attention from others

It's so common there is a gaggle of synonyms for it: bellyaching, grousing, moaning, nagging, nit-picking, scathing, grouching, fault-finding, and my favorite, griping."

William introduced me to Teddy Roosevelt. Following his advice, I devoured the Pulitzer Prize-winning biography *The Rise of Theodore Roosevelt* by Edmund Morris. T.R. quickly became one my all-time favorite heroes and mentors. I have devoured dozens of books since then about and by him (he wrote 31 books, all on different subjects, and spoke five languages!). When I learned that T.R. read a book a day, that inspired me to up my reading commitment.

This particular quote came from a speech he gave shortly before he died:

> *It is not the critic who counts: not the man who points out how the strong man stumbles or where the doer of deeds could have done better. The credit belongs to the man who is actually in the arena, whose face is marred by dust and sweat and blood, who strives valiantly, who errs and comes up short again and again, because there is no effort without error or shortcoming, but who knows the great enthusiasms, the great devotions, who spends himself in a worthy cause; who, at the best, knows, in the end, the triumph of high achievement, and who, at the worst, if he fails, at least he fails while daring greatly, so that his place shall never be with those cold and timid souls who knew neither victory nor defeat.*
>
> Theodore Roosevelt
> speech at the Sorbonne, Paris, April 23, 1910

Legendary basketball coach John Wooden once said, *"You can't let praise or criticism get to you. It's a weakness to get caught up in either one."*

I was complaining to William one day. He smiled, took a sip of tea, and said, "That's not to say I don't want feedback and learn about how I can improve what I do and who I am becoming. As long as it's from someone I admire who has my back and cares about me, then I am all for it. I want to change, improve, get better. It's the person who always complains, all the time, to everyone, I choose to avoid. An anchor is someone who drags me to the bottom. A speedboat is someone who pulls me forward. For my own sake and sanity, I need to differentiate between the two and adjust accordingly. Life is too short to spend time with people who belittle. Think about it, they are saying, 'BE-Little!' No sir, not for me."

He continued, "Sir Elton John once said, *"I'm not everybody's cup of tea. But sometimes criticism can be hurtful. Be respectful. I'm a good piano player, I can sing well, I write good songs. If you don't like it, fair enough. But give me a break."*

William paused to take a sip of his tea and then continued with the lesson. "Everyone is glad to see me, some when I arrive and some when I leave. I'm good either way! If you live for the compliments, you'll die by the criticism."

"So how do we handle the critic?" I asked.

"Context matters," he said. "If they are an anchor, consider the source, smile, wish them well, and walk away. If they persist, try saying, 'Let's agree to disagree. I'm choosing to go. Good luck ...' Graciously ghost them. Life is too short to invest time with people who just want to nit-pick, whine, and find validation."

I was writing notes in my journal as fast as I could. He paused so I could catch up. After a few sips of tea, he continued. "Watch out for the joy-stealers: gossip, criticism, complaints, fault-finding, and negative, judgmental attitudes. Criticism is prejudice made plausible. The final proof of greatness lies in being able to endure criticism without resentment."

Will Bowen wrote an amazing book and created a movement. In *A Complaint Free World: The 21-day challenge that will change your life* he explains why we gripe by turning it into an acronym: **G.R.I.P.E.**

G = Get attention
R = Remove responsibility
I = Inspire envy
P = Power play
E = Excuse poor performance

In his book he quotes Maya Angelou: *"If you don't like something, change it. If you can't change it, change your attitude. Don't complain."*

Have you ever tried to NOT complain or gossip for a day? It's harder than you think. "Remember," William said to me, "Thoughts held in the mind reproduce after their kind; What we resist, will persist; What you articulate you demonstrate!

"Here is a challenge from Will Bowen's book, "Can you go a whole day without complaining? How many times a day do you complain? Put a large English coin in your pocket. When you find yourself complaining aloud, stop, take the coin from one side and place it in the other pocket. See if you can not complain for 21 days!"

Before I could respond he said, "That's how long it takes to form a new positive habit. It took me three months to achieve my goal of a complaint-free life of 21 days without griping, complaining, or gossiping. It's one of the toughest things I ever tried to master."

"But what if I feel resentful toward a critic?" I asked.

"I consider the source," he said. "If they are someone I am forced to spend time with, like co-workers, family, vendors, etc., I pray for them and limit my time with them. Moreover, I change my expectations that I can change them in any meaningful and lasting way. They are who they are; it is what it is. Acceptance is simple, not easy."

Teddy was right. He also said, *"I like constructive criticism from smart people who care about my well-being; moreover, don't come to me with a complaint unless you have some solutions to offer!"*

Few people have the wisdom to prefer the criticism that would do them good to the praise that deceives them. Amen.

If it is not right do not do it; if it is not true do not say it.
Marcus Aurelius

4

On Gratitude

When I'm old I'll tell my tales, with all the gratitude I can muster,
And in keeping with Teddy Roosevelt, that famous trust-buster.

William told me a story. He was waiting in line at a grocery store in St. George, Utah. "I struck up a conversation with a woman who was eight months pregnant. She had two daughters in tow, ages four and six. The six-year-old was excited about going to a kindergarten open house. The four-year-old wanted to know when SHE was going to get to do that. I was struck by the phrase, "I'll be happy when ...

"I'll be happy when I am in first grade. I'll be happy when I get to junior high. I'll be happy when I get to high school. I'll be happy when I am in college ..."

I asked William to elaborate. He laughed and said, "When you are a child, happiness is always just a step away from where you are. In my senior year in high school, spring lasted forever. I couldn't wait to blow this pop stand and get to college to play ball. As parents, we say, *I can't wait until the baby is born. It will be so nice when the kids are out of diapers! Won't it be great when the kids are in school?* And so it goes ... 'I will be happy when ...' is a trap. It presupposes we are guaranteed happiness when we get to the next level. Believe me when I say that once your nest is empty, all you have left are love and memories, memories that many parents pine for, but they complained about when they were in the midst of them. Ironic, isn't it?

"Seriously, how do we avoid the trap of 'I'll be happy when?'" I asked. I could see he was getting ready to deliver a sermon worth remembering. I grabbed my journal to capture his ideas.

"'Someday Isle' is a lie we tell ourselves that robs us of the joy of the present," he said. "Hopelessly longing for something better down the road." He shared five strategies to enjoy the present:

1. **Have a Positive Expectation of the Future.** Expect to succeed. By all means, set challenging goals and work hard and smart to move toward them daily. At the same time, have purpose and meaning in your life and work, reasons to get out of bed in the morning. Choose optimism and really believe *The best is yet to come!*

2. **Be Grateful for What You Have NOW!** Make a list of the blessings you have right now. A healthy body, a clear mind, family, good friends, a roof over your head, a warm bed, and meaningful work. Remind yourself why this is the greatest country in the world. Choose to have an Attitude of Gratitude every day. It's a decision, a choice, a habit, and a philosophy of life. Melody Beattie wrote, *"Gratitude makes sense of our past, brings peace for today, and creates a vision for tomorrow. At times our own light goes out and is rekindled by a spark from*

another person. Each of us has cause to think with deep gratitude of those who have lighted the flame within us."

3. **Work Smart**. Plan your day on paper. Never walk out the door without well-thought-out marching orders. Invest in "The Hour of Power." For 20 minutes each, READ, THINK, PLAN. In addition: Go the extra mile. Give your customers and employer more than they expect from you. Under-promise and over-deliver! Ask yourself, *"How can I increase the quality and quantity of my service to others (on a daily basis!)?"* Chop wood, carry water.

4. **Savor Each Day**. Live each day as if it were your last. One day, you will be right, no regrets. It's called *the present* for a reason. Each day truly is a gift. Listen to Tim McGraw's song "Live Like You Were Dying" or "The Living Years" by Mike + The Mechanics as a reminder. Life is short. Forgive the people who have hurt you, forgive everyone you love and care about. Forgive and forget.

5. **Have Fun and Learn to Laugh Now**. Work hard, play hard, have fun, and remember to laugh every day. It heals the heart. It spreads joy. Herman Hesse said, *"All higher humor begins with ceasing to take oneself seriously."*

Someday Isle (I'll) is a lie. Someday the kids will be out of the house, then I'll be happy. Someday I'll go to Hawaii, Disneyland, Australia with my wife and kids. Someday I'll get to ... What if Someday doesn't arrive? Do it now. Take that vacation. What are you waiting for? I have never regretted a single trip I took (even when I felt like I couldn't take the time off or afford it).

If it's true that 68% of American men are dead within 18 months of retirement (and in my experience and observation, it is) why are you waiting to be happy? What if you did what you love? Took a risk? Nike was right. "Just do it!"

I'll be happy right now. I will embrace the day now. I will book that trip to "Someday Isle" today. What are you waiting for? *Tempus fugit* (Time flies). Enjoy the journey, don't miss the trip. Then pass it on ...

Pausing for a moment to gather his thoughts, William said, "I read *Unbroken* by Laura Hillenbrand in three days. I couldn't put it down. Adjectives to describe this reading experience: *Staggering, mesmerizing, meticulous, soaring, extraordinary, beautiful, powerful, startling.* Those words under-promise. While devouring it, I had an overwhelming flood of gratitude. It will make you cry, think, and laugh."

Alice Walker wrote, "'*Thank you' is the best prayer that anyone could say. I say that one a lot. Thank you expresses extreme gratitude, humility, understanding.*"

I wonder how that open house went for that little girl in Utah. I bet she can't wait for school to start in the fall. Me neither ...

Very little is needed to make a happy life;
it is all within yourself, in your way of thinking.
Marcus Aurelius

5

On Leading by Able Example

When I'm old I'll seek to inspire and lead by example,
And share the hard-won lessons of my past, perhaps just a sample.

My children never listened to a word I said, but they watched every move I made. I suspect that is true for all of us. An ounce of example is worth a pound of words. If our words and behavior are aligned, others will follow us. My parents were not perfect, no parents are. I do recall, when I was 12 years old, my father said to me, "Do what I say, not what I do." I knew that was flawed thinking, incongruent, and just plain wrong. I never forgot that.

William said to me one day as we were walking around Green Lake, "Think about the best coaches, teachers, and bosses you have had. Who had the most influence on you? Who inspired you the most? Who were you inspired to follow and listen to?"

Smiling, he continued "One of the most important things a leader can do is to lead by example. If you want everyone else to be passionate, committed, dedicated, and motivated, the true servant leader must go first! He or she must be the kind of person they would like others to become."

I replied, "I would say that my role model, as far as just somebody leading by example, would be my mum. She was self-taught, an autodidact, a voracious reader of books. She wrote a letter to her mum in England every day. She was a good person and definitely one of the biggest influences in my life. She kept a journal and constantly worked on becoming a better version of herself."

"She inspired you—by her able example?" William observed.

"Yes," I replied.

William proceeded to quote the poet Henry W. Longfellow.

Those heights by great men, won and kept,
Were not achieved by sudden flight.
But they, while their companions slept,
Were toiling upward in the night.

His recall for poetry was nothing short of extraordinary.

William then offered another gem from history. "Tom Edison is one of my heroes. His herculean work ethic was legendary. He rarely slept more than four hours a night. Edison may be the greatest inventor in history. He has over 1,000 patents to his name. Many of his inventions still have a major effect on our lives today. He was also a true business entrepreneur.

"Several of his inventions were group efforts in his laboratory where he had teams of people working in harmony to create, develop, build, and test his inventions. Edison used his inventions to form companies, including General Electric which is one of the biggest corporations in the world today."

Thomas Edison was born in Milan, Ohio on February 11, 1847. His family soon moved to Port Huron, Michigan where he spent most of his childhood. Surprisingly, he did not do well in school and ended up being home-schooled by his mother. It's been said he read every book in the Milan library by the time he was sixteen! Thomas was an enterprising young man, selling vegetables, candy, and newspapers on trains. One day he saved a child from a runaway train. The child's father repaid Edison's bravery by training him as a telegraph operator. In his new job, Thomas became interested in communications, which would be the focus of many of his inventions.

Few men or women in history led by example quite like Mr. Edison. His most famous patents include:

The Phonograph. This was Edison's first major invention and it made him both rich and famous. It was the first machine that was able to record and play back sound. Every musician since 1900 owes Mr. Edison a debt of gratitude. He invented an entire new industry: a way to buy and listen to music.

The Light Bulb. Although he did not invent the first electric light, Edison made the first practical electric light bulb that could be manufactured and used in the home and for business. He also invented other items that were needed to make the light bulb practical for use including safety fuses and on/off switches for light sockets. In other words, yet another entire industry!

The Motion Picture. Edison did a lot of work in creating the motion picture camera and helping move forward the progress of practical movies. Actors, take a bow and say thank you.

Fun Facts About Thomas Edison:
- His middle name was Alva and his family called him Al.
- His first two kids were nicknamed Dot and Dash.
- He set up his first lab in his parents' basement at the age of 10.
- He was partially deaf.

- His very first invention was an electric vote recorder.
- His 1,093 patents are the most on record.
- He recited the words to "Mary Had a Little Lamb" as the first recorded voice on the phonograph.

Do your words and actions match? Do you lead by example? I just turned off the stereo and the lights so I could watch a movie. Thanks, Tom ... for all three!

Waste no more time arguing about what a good man should be.
Be one.
Marcus Aurelius

6

On Rule 62

When I'm old I'll laugh at myself and follow Rule 62,
Because I always feel better, every time that I do.

I was speaking to 500 people in Orlando, Florida a few years ago. After the standing ovation (which, at the risk of sounding arrogant, never gets old) there was a long line at my "Back-of-the-Room Sales Table" for a book signing. One gentleman with a perpetual smile on his face waited patiently. When he finally reached me, as he handed me a twenty-dollar bill for his signed copy of *Freedom From Fear,* he exclaimed enthusiastically, "I love your self-*defecating* humor!" Sensing he was oblivious to his faux pas, I replied, "That's a shitty thing to say." As his light came on he said, "Oh crap!" I said, "Exactly! I knew what you meant. No worries. I appreciate the feedback." I gave him a book and said, "This one's on me!" as I handed back his money.

Self-*effacing* humor, the willingness and ability to make fun of yourself, is at the heart of Rule 62. It means, *Don't take yourself too seriously. Lighten up!* Life is too short to have thin skin and low self-esteem. Self-worth and humility are the twin towers of a healthy sense of self.

Self-worth is attached to self-esteem; that is to say, knowing you are good and wearing it well. Self-respect is how you feel about yourself when no one else is around. C.S. Lewis wrote, *"Humility is not thinking less of yourself; it's thinking of yourself less."*

William added to my evolving philosophy when he said to me, "When I poke fun of me, you don't get to. I tell the world that I'm comfortable in my own skin. I routinely make fun of my height, hairline, and grey hair. I say things like, *I have a face for radio. When the barber asks if I want him to 'trim the ears' he means inside!* When the day comes that you can take your assets and lofty position less seriously, it's like lancing a boil. It is its own relief. It's a healthy confidence combined with compassion for self."

My late great mentor Charlie "T." Jones used to say, "My book is in its eighth printing. It's because the first seven were blurred!" (Just for the record, he sold over 2,000,000 copies of *Life Is Tremendous*. He gave 200,000 away!)

The higher up you go in life, the more vital it is to embrace Rule 62. Life and business are about connection. When I make someone laugh WITH me, the connection grows stronger. Rapport happens in an instant. Why? Most people don't do it. It's as simple as that. I used to laugh AT others. Now I laugh WITH them, at myself.

When we laugh, a relaxation response comes over the body, mind, and heart. The most wasted of all days is one without laughter. Mark Twain once wrote, *"Humor is mankind's greatest blessing."* It's like a mini vacation. If I am feeling sorry for myself, I employ a few simple strategies:

1.   I make someone laugh using self-effacing humor.

2. I read something to make me laugh.
3. I watch a comedian on YouTube or a comedy.
4. I journal the absurdity of it all.
5. I listen to a podcast or Audible done by funny people.

William Arthur Ward wrote, *"A well-developed sense of humor is the pole that adds balance to your steps as you walk the tightrope of life."*

Victor Borge said, *"Laughter is the closest distance between two people."*

Groucho Marx said, *"Humor is reason gone mad."*

I recently had a travel day from hell. My flight from Charlotte to Atlanta was delayed for 90 minutes as we sat on the tarmac waiting for a lightning storm to pass us by. I missed my connection to Seattle. I rerouted to Austin and barely made my connection to Seattle (they were closing the gates as I ran through the terminal). Then my bag was taken by someone else at baggage claim. I got it the next day. During the drive home I ran over a muffler that had fallen off someone else's car. Instead of getting home at noon, I got home at 8 p.m. I was frustrated and feeling sorry for myself. So on the shuttle from the airport to the parking facility, I began entertaining the baby boomers on the bus and had them in stitches for ten minutes.

A woman asked me if I was a comedian. I said, "No, I'm a professional speaker and author. I just needed to change my mindset." She asked me how she could get a copy of one of my books. I handed her a copy of *A Simple Choice* and signed it. She was glowing. I felt better. Huh?

I'll keep following Rule 62. Because I always feel better when I do.

He who lives in harmony with himself
lives in harmony with the universe.
Marcus Aurelius

7

On Kíndness

When I'm old I'll practice kindness, of the radical variety,
Then, like Mr. Fred Rogers, I can positively impact society.

One evening, over dinner, I asked William, "Kindness. What exactly is that? Is it the same as being nice?"

Putting down his knife and fork (because he eats the British way with fork in the left hand and knife in the right), he began: "The best person to ask is the late great children's television host Mr. Fred Rogers. *Mr. Rogers*, as many children of my generation knew him, made a huge impact on the lives of millions of children. Through his ministry and his television show *Mister Rogers' Neighborhood*, he helped mentor and educate young children about the importance of kindness, tolerance, community, and friendship." The way William told a story, you couldn't look away and didn't want to be anywhere else. His delivery, facial expressions, intonation, even voices he used when he quoted a famous historical figure were riveting.

He flipped to a page in his journal and continued. "Here are some of my all-time favorite Mr. Rogers quotes.

Try your best to make goodness attractive. That's one of the toughest assignments you'll ever be given. What really matters is helping others win, too, even if it means slowing down and changing our course now and then.

We all have different gifts, so we all have different ways of saying to the world who we are. When I was a boy and I would see scary things in the news, my mother would say to me, 'Look for the helpers. You will always find people who are helping.'

In every neighborhood, all across our country, there are good people insisting on a good start for the young, and doing something about it. It always helps to have people we love beside us when we have to do difficult things in life.

All of us, at some time or other, need help. Whether we're giving or receiving help, each one of us has something valuable to bring to this world. That's one of the things that connects us as neighbors—in our own way, each one of us is a giver and a receiver.

There are three ways to ultimate success:
The first way is to be kind.
The second way is to be kind.
The third way is to be kind."

He continued, "We live in a world in which we desperately need to share responsibility for our fellow man. It's easy to say, 'It's not my child, not my community, not my world, not my problem.' Then

36

there are those who see the need and do respond. Their mantra is 'I am Responsible.' I consider those people my heroes. No one else can live the life you live. And even though no human being is perfect, we always have the chance to bring what's unique about us to live in a redeeming way."

Shifting gears, he leaned in and lowered his voice. "I hope you're proud of yourself for the times you've said 'Yes,' when all it meant was extra work for you and was seemingly helpful only to somebody else. The world needs a sense of worth, and it will achieve it only by its people feeling that they are worthwhile. Anyone who does anything to help a child in his or her life is a hero to me."

As if to say *PS,* he ended with, "Nice comes from the head, kind comes from the heart."

His message that day had me really looking inward. Then I said, "So you are saying it's our job to encourage each other to discover that uniqueness and to provide ways of developing its expression? To love someone is to strive to accept that person exactly the way he or she is, right here and now with love? That's kindness in action?"

"Indeed," was all he said. That night there was no reason for dessert, I was full ... of joy and a yearning to be kinder.

That night I went through an old journal from 2003. I was in Pittsburgh conducting a seminar and enjoying reading a local Pennsylvania newspaper. The cover story was about hometown hero Fred Rogers. It was a three-page spread on his life and contribution:

Fred McFeely Rogers, better known as Mister Rogers, was an American television host, author, producer, and Presbyterian minister. He was the creator, showrunner, and host of the preschool television series Mister Rogers' Neighborhood, which ran for an unprecedented 33 years, from 1968 to 2001. He was a stand-up guy and a pioneer in human relations.

Rest in peace, Fred. You were as kind as they come. The very definition of the word in action and attitude.

The newspaper profile ended with this thought: *"Imagine what our neighborhoods would be like if each of us offered, as a matter of course, just one kind word to another person."*

We ought to do good to others as simply as a horse runs, or a bee makes honey, or a vine bears grapes season after season without thinking of the grapes it has borne.
Marcus Aurelius

8

On Listening and Understanding

When I'm old I'll listen more, to everyone I meet,
From the butcher, baker, and candlestick maker
to the CEO on Wall Street.

One fine day I was reading an article in *The New Yorker* when a light went off in my head. The author was talking about the importance of listening actively to clients and friends. A few days later, I stumbled across an out-of-print book by Wendell Johnson entitled *Your Enchanted Listener.*

The next day, William asked me over the phone, "By the way, have you ever studied active listening?"

"Why no," I replied.

Before I could gather my response he asked, "Have you ever read any Carl Rogers?"

"No, but ..."

William said, "Indeed." It was a short conversation. Message delivered, message received. I ordered the book *Active Listening* by Carl Rogers and read it one sitting.

I find it fascinating how the universe delivers just the right information from just the right people at just the right time, when we are ready for it. *The old saw, When the student is ready to learn, the teacher(s) show up!* is so true.

I combined what I had recently learned from William's book suggestion, the article, and from Mr. Johnson. It was like discovering plutonium by accident. I just knew I had uncovered something magical. I decided to test it.

I wrote out a 3x5 goal card that said, ***I dominate the listening in every conversation and people enjoy being around me. I consistently listen actively to others!"***

It changed my life.

A few weeks later I created this formula:

Active Listening = L.P.Q.P.

L*isten Actively*

P*ause 3-5 seconds*

Q*uestion for Clarification*

P*araphrase for Understanding*

This is one of those habits that is hard to form but easy to live with. As I began to experiment I made a few observations in my journal:

As a doctor, before you can prescribe, you must diagnose!

Forget 'Closing the sale'! This is about 'Opening the relationship'!

Spurred on by what I had been learning from my experiments, I began to play a game with people I met on airplanes, in coffee shops, or standing in line at the bank or post office, to test my new theory. I wondered if I could get a stranger to talk about themselves for 15-20 minutes without them knowing they have been doing all the talking. You see, my senior year of high school I was voted "Most Talkative" by my graduating class. It wasn't a compliment. My older brother used to say to me when I was a kid, "I'll give you a quarter if you can be quiet for 20 minutes!" I never did get the two bits.

As an adult, and as a professional salesperson at the time, using this simple method, the quarters began to fall into my lap like manna from heaven. It was magic. Even when my new friends realized what I was doing, they didn't seem to care. It turns out NO ONE LISTENS! Let me repeat that: NO ... ONE ... LISTENS! Well, almost no one.

When you become the person who does actively listen, people will want to spend time with you but won't know why! They will simply like how you make them feel. It's simple but not easy. Ego, fear, pride all conspire to undermine this new positive-listening habit. It requires a kind of dying of self, a commitment to "other-centeredness." What if you don't get to talk? Would you rather be right or rich?

I can't tell you how many friends I have made of strangers, how many deals I have closed because I didn't speak, just listened, with intention and sincerity.

At its core, it's a theory of living, a way of being, a philosophy.

William bought his suits from a fellow at the Seattle Nordstrom, from sales superstar and author Pat McCarthy. He said, "He taught me, be 'OTHER-centered.' It's a combination of empathy, compassion, and active listening. It's so simple. It's just not easy. It's hard at first, like folding your arms the wrong way. When it is finally my turn to speak, I usually tell a story. The story summarizes their pain, contains a solution to their challenges. In their minds, they think, 'That's what I want.'" William was a true student and he borrowed boldly from the best.

Larry King said, *"I remind myself every morning: Nothing I say this day will teach me anything. So if I'm going to learn, I must do it by listening."*

Margret Wheatley said, *"Listening is such a simple act. It requires us to be present, and that takes practice, but we don't have to do anything else. We don't have to advise, or coach, or sound wise. We just have to be willing to sit there and listen."*

William challenged me with a few simple questions: "How about you? What if you made active listening a habit? A way of being?"

This new path led me to another acronym: **W.A.I.T.**

W.A.I.T. stands for **W**hy **A**m **I** **T**alking?

Why indeed? Now I was using that word ... *indeed.*

When I shared my newfound insights with William, he asked, "What if you dominated the listening in <u>every</u> conversation? What percentage of the time are you listening to your child, your spouse, your friends, or your prospects? Many years ago I asked myself a simple question: Why not set a goal to dominate the listening and try it for a month? 30 days. That is how long it takes to form a new positive habit. First we form habits, then habits form us. One thing is certain after thirty years of this 'other-centered philosophy' in action—at the risk of repeating myself, if I dominate the listening, people will want to spend more time with me but won't know why. They will just like how I make them feel. Moreover, they will tell me things they don't tell their barber, banker, or best friend!"

Kate Murphy, author of *You're Not Listening: What You're Missing and Why It Matters,* wrote, *"To listen well is to figure out what's on someone's mind and demonstrate that you care enough to want to know. It's what we all crave; to be understood as a person with thoughts, emotions, and intentions that are unique and valuable and* deserving of attention. *Listening is about the experience of being experienced. It's when someone takes an interest in who you are and what you are doing."*

Maybe it's time to write that goal out again on a 3x5 card. I still talk too much! I could really use a quarter ...

To understand the true quality of people, you must look into their minds, and examine their pursuits and aversions.

Marcus Aurelius

9

On Cynics and Whiners

When I'm old I'll exercise my right to walk away
From the cynics and the whiners, before they wreck my day.

What is a cynic? The dictionary definition is *a person who believes that people are motivated purely by self-interest rather than acting for honorable or unselfish reasons.* A cynic might think the governor visited the hospital just to gain votes. In other words, any person described as a detractor, doubting Thomas, skeptic, or pessimist falls into this category.

William told me a story during a long drive to a speaking engagement. "Martin Seligman is a pioneer in the arena of optimism. He contends, *'If you were an optimistic teen, then you will be an optimist at 80 years young.'* He also posits, *'It's not a surprise that optimistic athletes, managers and teams perform better. What's interesting is <u>where</u> they do better. It's in coming back from defeat and* *adversity to acting in the clutch!'* But my favorite quote of his is *'Optimistic people generally feel that good things will last a long time and will have a beneficial effect on everything they do. Moreover, they think that bad things are isolated; they won't last long and won't affect other parts of their life. Pessimists think the exact opposite, that is, bad things will last a long time, have negative effects on everything they do and they have no control over the outcome, in other words, victimhood.'"*

William said to me, "I'm not a cynic. What about whiners? Hey, if I am honest, I whine sometimes. Yep, you heard it right. That's a tough pill to swallow because I have invested over 40 years, better than half my adult life, trying to overcome a challenging childhood. So why do I whine? For some of the same reasons you do:

1. Attention
2. Affection
3. Solace
4. To get it off our chest
5. Sympathy

As we discussed previously, Teddy Roosevelt said, *"Complaining about a problem without posing a solution is called whining!"*

John Waters, the flamboyant director, said it best: *"Life can be for some of us a rotten lottery. I've had a pretty amazing life, a good life and God knows I'm thankful; but I do believe that after age 30, as an adult, stop whining! Everybody's dealt a hard hand from time to time and it's not fair what you get. But you've got to deal with it."*

William said to me, as we pulled into the hotel parking lot, "In the end, it's not what happens to me, rather how I respond. Look, I have survived bankruptcy, life-threatening surgery twice, two car accidents where my car was totaled, and almost falling seven stories on a construction site but for a co-worker grabbing my arm just in time to turn me around. Life is dangerous and, for most of us, short. Yes, one could argue life isn't fair, it's true, yet I still need to deal with it. Whining about it rarely levels the playing field, but learning to rise above it is the ultimate reward."

It's not how far we fall, rather how high we bounce that counts. I don't know how many more Sundays I have left. I'm hoping and striving for 1,560 (that will take me to 95 years young like William!). But I know one thing for certain, I'm going to continue to edit my reactions and curb my affinity for a pessimistic viewpoint because I want to be able to say to my grandchildren, "You want some cheese with your whine?" and not have them say to me, "Do YOU?"

When I come across someone who consistently demonstrates a penchant for whining, I reserve the right to walk away. Birds of a feather really do flock together. Eagles don't hang around seagulls.

I also make it a point to avoid "The News." Have you ever noticed there's always "BREAKING NEWS" scrolling across the bottom of the TV screen? And it's always Breaking BAD News! In my worldview, CNN stands for *Constant Negative News*. I'm learning to manage my input. G.I.G.O. Stands for *Garbage In, Garbage Out*. No news is good news. I do read *The New York Times,* but I limit it to the business, sports, and entertainment sections.

I love my life. I consider myself an "optimistic stoic" and a work in progress. My life is about progress, not perfection. Love and tolerance is my code. One day at a time ...

There is nothing that happens to any person
but what was in his power to go through with.
Marcus Aurelius

10

On Laughter

When I'm old I'll make people laugh and tickle their funny bone,
So that their heart's made lighter and they will never feel alone.

A ndrew Carnegie was worth 600 million dollars at the time of his death in 1919 at age 84. He once said, *"There is little success where there is little laughter."*

Laughter is an instant vacation. It heals the soul. It releases endorphins into our system and a relaxation response comes over the body. Besides, laughter and tears are both responses to frustration and exhaustion. I, myself, prefer to laugh, since there is less cleaning up to do afterward! It is impossible for you to be angry and laugh at the same time. Anger and laughter are mutually exclusive and you have the power to choose either.

One of my favorite writers is Stephen King. His stories are dark, ominous, and downright scary, yet he once said, *"You can't deny laughter; when it comes, it plops down in your favorite chair and stays as long as it wants."*

William told me another story about his favorite comic, Rodney "No Respect" Dangerfield as we walked the beach near his home. "His childhood life was heartbreaking. An alcoholic, bitter mother, an absentee, philandering father, made for an incredibly sad childhood. They were so poor, when he was nine years old, he found a job selling ice cream at the beach and made and managed to save over 100 dollars in 1932. That was real money back then, a princely sum. When he went to the bank to take some out, he found that his mother had stolen ALL of it. 'We needed it,' was all she said. In true Rodney form, he shrugged it off and proceeded to find a different way to earn some dough.

"His comedy came from his pain. He said, *'I lived in a tough neighborhood growing up. There was an Italian restaurant near my house, Nunzio's, formerly Vito's, which served broken leg of lamb. These guys were tough.'*

"His story is unique. He started doing stand-up in New York at 16. Then, at 28, he left the industry to sell aluminum siding for 12 years. He had a family. At forty, he jumped back into comedy with both feet. He passed away at 82. He was an icon. He found the respect he never received as a child."

"So humor heals the receiver but not necessarily the sender. That is work that is separate from the delivery of it?" I asked.

"Indeed. But why do comedy and humor heal the receiver? According to Dr. William Fry, professor emeritus at Stanford University School of Medicine, *'Each humor event you experience makes you grow a little bit. As the brain has expanded, it takes on new connections.'* Humor improves memory. Advertisers have known this for years. Otherwise, we wouldn't have lizards selling insurance or dogs selling beer. *'Humor loosens up the mind and fosters creativity and innovation,'* according to Dr. Alice Isen, a professor of psychology and management at Cornell University."

There is something special about a walk and talk, especially on the beach. William continued, "Norm Cousins, in his book *The Healing Heart,* used himself as the guinea pig. Describing the power of humor and laughter which bolsters the immune system, he coined the term *psycho-neuro-immunology.* He was diagnosed with a fatal illness and given a 10% chance of survival. He walked out of the hospital six weeks later healthy as a horse. His remedy? Massive doses of vitamin C and vitamin H (humor). He watched dozens of comedies, over and over—the Marx Brothers, the Three Stooges, Hope and Crosby, Martin and Lewis, Abbott and Costello. Next time you feel sorry yourself, go to a comedy club, listen to a podcast by a comedian, watch a comedy like *Wedding Crashers* or *Sleepless in Seattle,* or pick up a good humor book like Nora Ephron's masterpiece, *I Feel Bad About My Neck* or Billy Crystal's *700 Sundays* or *The Thunderbolt Kid* by Bill Bryson, and have a good laugh. Better yet, read it to a friend who is feeling blue and make milk come out of their nose. You will feel better, I promise!"

I'm thankful for laughter, except when milk comes out of *my* nose.

And thou wilt give thyself relief,
if thou doest every act of thy life as if it were the last.
Marcus Aurelius

11

On the Letter

When I'm old I'll write that letter,
To the teachers who believed in me,
So that they'll know they made a difference in all I do and see.

It was rare that William invested more than 10-15 minutes telling me his amazing stories. It usually meant we went for a short walk or had a cup of tea at a little independent coffee shop. This night, we had a long dinner at the Painted Table, a five-star restaurant with white table cloths. I asked him about his father; and so began a long story, one I had never heard before. His face turned solemn as he leaned forward and began ...

"A letter was found in Abraham Lincoln's desk, posthumously. It was an 'angry unsent letter,' or an A.U.L. Evidently, he wrote more than a few of them. Shortly after the Battle of Gettysburg, Lincoln composed one such letter to General George Meade in which he expressed profound disappointment in Meade's inability to pursue and destroy Robert E. Lee's army. Lincoln did not send the letter—writing such correspondence and storing it away was a favorite coping mechanism of his." William opened his journal and unfolded a piece of paper. "In the interest of time, I'll skip to the last paragraph.

Again, my dear general, I do not believe you appreciate the magnitude of the misfortune involved in Lee's escape—He was within your easy grasp, and to have closed upon him would, in connection with our other late successes, have ended the war—As it is, the war will be prolonged indefinitely. If you could not safely attack Lee last Monday, how can you possibly do so South of the river, when you can take with you very few more than two thirds of the force you then had in hand? It would be unreasonable to expect, and I do not expect you can now effect much. Your golden opportunity is gone, and I am distressed immeasurably because of it—I beg you will not consider this a prosecution, or persecution of yourself; As you had learned that I was dissatisfied, I have thought it best to kindly tell you why.

To Gen. Meade, never sent, or signed."

Shifting gears, William's tone changed to one of sincerity, almost a whisper, like he didn't want anyone else to hear. "One frustrating day, I wrote an angry unsent letter to my mother and father. I was 38 years old. I vented all the frustrations I had at the time, like so many new parents who deal with challenges of overbearing grandparents. I held nothing back. I printed it and showed it to my wife. She smiled and said, 'It was really important that you wrote this letter. Now, it is even more important that you NEVER send it.'" Great advice.

"15 Years later, my mother was struggling with cancer. I wrote a very different kind of letter." William pulled out another piece of paper. "I called it *Ten Great Things I Admire about You, Barbara Jean Oldham!*

1. *You make a great cup of tea. (She was very British!)*
2. *You and Dad stayed together through thick and thin (and there was a lot of thin!) for over 55 years!*
3. *You are the glue that binds together all the diverse personalities in our crazy family, the voice of reason and objectivity.*
4. *You love to read, especially books, fiction and non-fiction, all from the library. You passed that gift on to me and my boys.*
5. *You are a woman of letters; writing them every day, old-school, with pen and paper, envelopes, and stamps. Always heartfelt and kind.*
6. *Your English accent is very charming and people enjoy being around you. You were always very polite, very proper, very British, even when others were not.*
7. *You were a wonderful "nanny" to our boys. They loved how you made their overnight visits special and all about them.*
8. *You took pictures of our boys and put them in binders and gave them to us as a way to remember lovely visits to bucolic Whidbey Island. We cherish those memories.*
9. *You made a dollar stretch like no one I ever knew. Cutting coupons, saving money, frugal, and ultimately you became financially independent, by some standards wealthy.*
10. *Did I mention the tea? You had rules about making it. It's why you never used a microwave. There are some things that just aren't done.*

"She called me a couple of weeks later and said, '*I received your letter parcel-post yesterday. It made me cry, Luv. I've shown it to all my friends. Thank you, William. You are a good son.*

"Now I made my mother cry a lot when I was a young boy, but not tears of joy!"

William stopped and took a drink of water, then continued. "The impact on my relationship with her was made so positively profound, I made a list of all the people who had made a difference in my life, my wife, our boys, old friends from childhood, teachers, coaches, mentors, it's a long list. One by one, I wrote a similar letter to each person, thinking deeply about their able example, positive qualities, and how they helped shape who I had become.

"In every instance and with every person, the relationship became stronger, deeper, and closer. In considering the WHY of it, I came to a few simple conclusions:

1. It validates their life and contribution.
2. We only ever hear about the negative things about ourselves from most people.
3. It was written on paper with ink, a stamp, and love—the palest ink is better than the strongest memory.
4. It took some time and thoughtful consideration—each one tailored to the person's strengths and qualities.
5. No one had ever done that for them, ever.
6. Everyone we meet is looking for three things: appreciation, respect, and understanding.
7. It's so simple and takes less time than you might think.

"Slowly but surely, this habit, this positive-affirmation of life, began to shape and inform all my interactions with the people I cared about. I began texting, emailing, and telling people verbally how I felt about the difference their caring actions and attitudes had made in my life.

"If you are blessed enough to have a favorite school teacher who used tough love to inspire you, as I did, that just might be a great place to start this process, as a kind of test. My German teacher, Susan Hall, was one such teacher for me. One day she said to me, 'William, you are better than this!' after I had acted out in class. Pulling me aside she affirmed, 'I expect more from you. You are a leader. Where you go, others follow. I can't have you cracking jokes in my class. Save that for the dialogues we do. Is it a deal?' 'It's a deal,' I replied. I earned an A every semester in her class. She knew what I needed before I ever did. She enrolled me in a pen-pal letter list. Seemingly out of the blue, I began to receive letters from girls my age from both Germany and England. I wrote letters every week for over two years. Perhaps that is when the seeds of becoming a writer were planted. It's only fitting that the very first time I wrote out my list of *Great Things I Got from You* was to Susan. I was speaking to 500 contractors in Yuma, Arizona. Halfway through my talk, I posted a slide that said, *Five Great Things I Got from Susan Hall.* She was in attendance and I introduced her to my audience. I read the five things and she got a standing ovation. The seeds I planted grew into a glorious flower bed.

"I was having breakfast at a lovely diner in North Bend, Washington with our oldest son and his wonderful wife. My granddaughter Penelope *Jean* (my mother's name) insisted on sitting next to me. She was five years old. Just before we ordered, I turned to her and said, '*Penny, you are SO beautiful, SO kind, SO athletic, SO smart ...*' She cut me off and said, '*Okay, that's enough. Let's order!*'

"Okay maybe five years old is too young to try this—and hey, it's not a letter. The spoken word is like frost on a windshield. It's gone in few minutes—but a letter ...

"When my father-in-law, Bob Babbington's, health was failing, he was 86 years old. I knew it was time to write him **The Letter.**

Dear Bob,

As I reflect upon the last 35 years, I can't help but be grateful for all you have done for me and my family. When I was at my absolute bottom, you and Ericka took me in, treated me as your son and changed my life forever. I will be forever in your debt for your over-whelming and unconditional love.

Here is my list of gifts you gave me by your able example. I call it **'10 Great Things I Got from You!'** *In no particular order:*

1) *How you showed your love to your family. You spelled love T-I-M-E. Camping, eating brunch, or dinner out, watching movies, going to church, always together.*

2) *You took the time to show me how to change the oil in my car and tune it up. Hours on the cold asphalt showing me how to set the timing. You were such a patient teacher.*

3) *You giving up the alcohol and cigarettes. I know first-hand how hard that is. It showed real commitment and love, the most unselfish act of all, and inspired me to do the same.*

4) *You went to church on Sunday. My family never did that. You were always teachable, humble, kind.*

5) *Hard work. You drove a truck for all those years, a thankless and unglamorous job, to provide for your family. By able example you showed me what a man is supposed to do.*

6) *Meaningful and thoughtful cards on my birthday. What you wrote was spot-on and well-thought-out. You took the time to say just the right thing. That always meant something to me.*

7) *Thoughtful gifts that demonstrated real caring and effort. Gifts that were MADE by hand and were specific to me and my life. Real creativity and love in each one.*

8) *Empathy. Your caring and kindness was and is extraordinary. You are a good soul.*

9) *Integrity. You always kept your word. I cannot think of a single time you broke a promise. You always showed up when you said you would. We could count on you.*

10) *Loyalty. Through all my ups and downs, you were always there, not just for your family, but for me.*

Shakespeare said it best in Hamlet: *'Doubt thou the stars are fire; Doubt that the sun doth move; Doubt truth to be a liar; But never doubt I love YOU.'*
I love you, Bob. You made a difference in my life and left an extraordinary legacy in your grandchildren. Thank you for showing me the way.
Your Grateful son-in-law, William Ian Oldham (W.I.O.)

"My sister-in-law called a week later and said, 'I just had lunch with Dad. He asked me to read the letter you wrote aloud. I did. He said it's the nicest thing anyone has ever done for him. He wants you to read it at his memorial.' A year later, read it I did.

"At Bob's memorial there wasn't a dry eye in the house. Ten different men came up to me afterward to thank me. One elderly gentleman in the most somber tone said, 'I hope and pray that, someday, someone writes a letter like that to me before I go.' I replied, 'Hey, we are all gonna go! Why not start the positive chain reaction of appreciation, respect, and understanding?'"

I was taking notes, oblivious to the fact I was in a five-star restaurant writing furiously to capture the key points from this amazing story.

Over dessert, pausing for effect, William continued, almost as if he was letting me get caught up. "But what if *you* made a list of the people who impacted your life in a positive way, and made the time, one by one, to write that letter? It doesn't have to be 10 things, it can be five. What matters is the *intent*. What matters are the *words*. What matters is the *meaning*. What matters is the *validation*. What matters is the *proof,* proof that this person matters to you and made a difference in your life.

"William James, the father of modern psychology, once wrote, *'The deepest craving in the human condition is the need to be appreciated.'* He used the word craving. We all crave appreciation, respect and understanding. The *10 Great Things* letter accomplishes all three elements in one fell swoop.

"Without realizing it, we set in motion a kind of positive chain reaction of love and affirmation that changes the hearts and minds of the people who matter to us most. Shortly after writing that letter to our oldest son, Colin, he gave me a precious gift for Christmas. It was a journal with thirty questions he had to answer by his own hand. It clearly took him some time to complete. It's called *I Love My Dad (and Here Is Why!)* It was lovely. He reminded me about so many things that had happened as a parent that I had forgotten about, that in hindsight were uproariously funny or bittersweet. It's the most precious book in my library."

The waiter brought the check. I reached for it before William could pay. "I got this," I said. He smiled.

"One last story for the night," I said. Now it was William's turn to listen. He leaned in so as not to miss a word.

"England in 1967 was a magical place. My mother was born and raised in Hillingdon, a short train ride from London. I was ten years old. My father, a retired Air Force vet, was sitting poolside reading his paper, as was his custom. I was in heaven in the Brighton pool, it was the size of a football field. There were three diving options: a regular diving board, a ten-foot board with tremendous spring, and the daunting 30-foot-high dive platform. To a ten-year-old it might as well have been 300 feet! I gathered up the courage to jump. It was the most exciting and exhilarating experience of my young life. I swam over to my father and said, 'Dad, I am going to go off the high dive (again). Watch!' You see, I was looking for what every ten-year-old longs for, to hear those two magic words from their father, *love* and *proud*. Standing at the edge, I looked over to make certain he was watching. I jumped. Just before I hit the water, I glanced back over only to see he had gone back to reading his paper. I hit the water. The hole in my stomach remained long after that moment. *I must not be good enough, or he would have watched,* I thought. I carried that erroneous belief for many years.

"When my children were young, we owned a lovely home with a sweeping view of Puget Sound, Mt. Baker's snow-capped peak, and—a swimming pool with a diving board. Evan, our youngest son, was three years old. He and I had been splashing around the shallow end, he with his little water wings and me with a great deal of patience and love. We spelled love TIME. He went into the house to get a bite to eat; I sat in the shallow end of the pool reading the Sunday *New York Times*. Lost in an article, I heard a little voice say, 'Dad, watch!' I looked up. There was Evan on the diving board with a Chesire Cat grin, waiting. 'Evan,' I said, 'are you going to go off the board into the deep end for the first time?' Smiling broadly, he replied, 'Yeaaahhh!' I sat up, folded my newspaper, and SAT on it. I wanted him to know I was watching and what he was about to do was important to me! He jumped. When he came out of the water, he breached like a whale. His grin started slowly, then went all the way up to the bottom of his ears. It was the biggest smile I had ever seen.

"He <u>saw</u> that I was watching. He swam over to me, jumped into my arms, hugged my neck, and kissed my cheek. 'Evan, that was awesome. I am so proud of you, son. I love you so much!' Evan looked at me, melting my heart with, 'Thanks, Dad. I love you, too.' In that moment, the sins of my father were healed. I was able to forgive him for his sins of omission and commission. You see, like all parents, my father did the best he could with what he knew. I was able to let that pain go, all from the love of a child. Not giving a thought to the consequence of the next phrase, I made a big mistake. I said, 'Do it again.' He did ... over and over and over. For the next hour, it's all he did."

William smiled. He knew the message had been received and understood. He said, "William James wrote, *'Action seems to follow feeling, but really action and feeling go together; and by regulating the action, which is under the more direct control of the will, we can indirectly regulate the feeling, which is not. Thus, the sovereign voluntary path to cheerfulness, if our spontaneous cheerfulness be lost, is to sit up cheerfully and to act and speak as if cheerfulness were already there. If such conduct does not make you feel cheerful, nothing else on that occasion can. So to feel brave, act as if we were brave, use all of our will to that end and a courage-fit will very likely replace the fit of fear.'"*

"In other words, *act as if,* and the feelings will follow?" I said.

"Indeed! Your son was brave," he exclaimed.

I continued, "A few weeks after my poolside epiphany my father came over to the house for Father's Day. Evan ran and jumped up into his arms and kissed his cheek. 'I love you, Boppa!' he exclaimed. My father melted. He smiled and replied, 'I love you too, Evan.' His force field was down. This was the first time those words had ever crossed his lips. He looked at me with an expression I had never seen before and said, 'I love you too, son. You are a good father. No one can say otherwise.'"

"That, young man, is a beautiful story!" William added, "I never got to write "The Letter" to my father before Alzheimer's took his mind and life."

I went from laughter to tears. William had passed his gift for telling a heartfelt story to me. Now, for the first time, I had infected him with the gift of story. This was one for the ages.

William took the figurative microphone back and said, "If you are waiting for a loved one to make the first move, don't. Life is short. Tell the people you care about how you feel. Write that letter. Forgive their sins, slights, and missteps. Let those old resentments go. Take the initiative before it's too late. Remember, everyone you meet is looking for three things: appreciation, respect, and understanding."

I remember thinking about what I would give for one more day with my dad. When he died I was old enough to remember everything but young enough to understand none of it.

I need to call my son.

The clock is ticking. I am going to write those letters. Don't put it off another day. Life is short.

Evidently, on her death bed, Abe Lincoln's mother's dying words were, "Abe, be somebody." Near the end of his life, he said, "All that I am, or hope to be, I owe to my angel mother." Amen, Abe.

As we left the Painted Table, I turned to William and said, "I've got some letters to write. Thank you, William." He just smiled, then said, "Indeed."

Death, like birth, is a secret of Nature.
Marcus Aurelius

12

On Reading

When I'm old I'll read the Bible and the 100 Greatest Books,
Alone on my deck with a cup of tea, ignoring the dirty looks.

William lived on the beach. We were sitting on his deck enjoying a cup of tea. He told me another story. "One spring morning, I found myself in the Nashville Airport after having completed a successful keynote. I was still basking in the glow of a standing ovation and having sold over 200 books. I had 150 names to enter into my e-newsletter database. I was typing away. My phone rang. It was my speaker friend, Kevin. He asked where I was and what I was doing. 'Oh, just entering some names into my database in the Nashville Airport.' There was a long pause—then Kevin said, *'Why are you doing that? That's a ten-dollar-an-hour job! Pay someone to do that so you can be reading a book instead!'* Ouch! He was right. That was ten years ago. That's Kevin. He is a Speedboat who cares. I've never entered another name since. I pay someone to do it. Since that day, I've read more than two books a week!"

"So your friend put a rock in your shoe and you had a shift in awareness that changed your life!" I said. *What a gift,* I thought.

"Indeed," William said. Gathering himself as if to say, *Where was I?* He continued. "As I have said before, Teddy Roosevelt is one of my heroes. He had an extraordinary love of learning. He read a book a day! He spoke German and French. That skill came in handy when he charged up San Juan Hill in Cuba and captured a German soldier who was manning a machine gun that didn't work. The wounded soldier told them how to use the gun as T.R. translated German to English. It was the turning point in the battle.

"He captured the hill. That was a watershed moment in the Spanish-American War. That made him famous. He was a true American hero. Moreover, he truly cared about his men. He memorized 1,250 Rough Rider's names! He would wander the camp at night encouraging his men, asking questions, and listening to their concerns. To shift their focus from the fear of the next battle, he often asked, '*What are you looking forward to after the war?*' Brilliant."

I responded by recalling a quote from one of my favorite writers, Oscar Wilde. He once wrote, *"If one cannot enjoy reading a book over and over again, there is no use in reading it at all."'*

William smiled. "I love that quote. He was a brilliant man." He opened his journal and proceeded to read from it.

"What follows are my favorite books since that day in the airport; many of these books I have read more than once.

1) *Freedom from Fear,* by Mark Matteson
2) *Creative Visualization,* by Shakti Gawain
3) *Mindset,* by Carol Dweck
4) *Chop Wood, Carry Water,* by Joshua Medcalf
5) *Think and Grow Rich,* by Napoleon Hill
6) *How to Win Friends and Influence People* by Dale Carnegie
7) *Born to Run,* by Bruce Springsteen

8) *A Year of Living Kindly,* by Donna Cameron
9) *Born Standing Up,* by Steve Martin
10) *The Rise of Theodore Roosevelt,* by Edmund Morris
11) *Broken Music,* by Sting
12) *On Writing,* by Stephen King
13) *Body for Life,* by Bill Phillips
14) *It's About TIME,* by Mark Matteson
15) *The Culture Code,* by Daniel Coyle
16) *Good to Great,* by Jim Collins
17) *Mind Gym,* by Gary Mack
18) *Wooden on Leadership,* by John Wooden
19) *Atomic Habits,* by James Clear
20) *The Talent Code,* by Daniel Coyle
21) *Marketing Your Dreams,* by Pat Williams
22) *Unbroken,* by Laura Hillenbrand
23) *Raising Positive Kids in a Negative World,* by Zig Ziglar
24) *How to Sell Anything to Anybody,* by Joe Girard
25) *Learned Optimism,* by Martin Seligman
26) *A Complaint Free World,* by Will Bowen
27) *Seven Spiritual Laws of Success,* by Deepak Chopra
28) *The Godfather,* by Mario Puzo
29) *The Unknown Lincoln,* by Dale Carnegie
30) *The Long Goodbye,* by Raymond Chandler
31) *Acres of Diamonds,* by Russell Conwell
32) *How to Read a Person Like a Book,* by Gerard Nierenberg
33) *Nasty People,* by Jay Carter
34) *Moby-Dick,* by Herman Melville
35) *The History of the Decline and Fall of the Roman Empire,*
    by Edward Gibbon
36) *The Essays of Emerson,* by Ralph Waldo Emerson
37) *Of Mice and Men,* by John Steinbeck
38) *The Old Man and the Sea,* by Ernest Hemingway
39) *Hamlet,* by William Shakespeare

40) *A Tale of Two Cities,* by Charles Dickens
41) *Adventures of Huckleberry Finn,* by Mark Twain
42) *The Bible* (*Proverbs, Galatians,* and *Matthew* are my favorites)
43) *The Picture of Dorian Gray,* by Oscar Wilde
44) *Robinson Crusoe,* by Daniel Defoe
45) *Pygmalion,* by George Bernard Shaw
46) *The Autobiography of Benjamin Franklin,*
     by Benjamin Franklin
47) *Aesop's Fables,* by Aesop
48) *Animal Farm,* by George Orwell
49) *Walden,* by Henry David Thoreau
50) *The Last of the Mohicans,* by James Fenimore Cooper"

"Wow, that is some list! I especially liked those books by Mark Matteson!" I said with a combination of modesty and sarcasm.

William laughed aloud and continued, "Ben Franklin advised, *'Either write something worth reading or do something worth writing about!'* Why not choose a book from this list and read for 20-30 minutes a day? Your life will never be the same."

"I guess I've got some reading to do," I said.

William smiled. "Indeed."

To understand the true quality of people, you must look into their minds, and examine their pursuits and aversions.
Marcus Aurelius

13

On Love

When I'm old I'll say I love you to every friend and foe,
Because life is so short, it must be said before I go.

When William wanted to grow in a particular area, he would read ten books on the subject and interview dozens of people who possessed the quality or characteristic he sought, then he would write about what he learned. I took a page from his book of lifelong learning and wrote the following:

What is love? The Greek word *Agape's* origin is the verb *agapan,* which means, *to greet with affection* or *to love!* It's the fourth love, and perhaps the most radical or selfless love. This is a love that you extend to all people, whether family members or distant strangers. Agape was later translated into Latin as *caritas,* which is the origin of our word *charity.* There it is. Charity. Brotherly love.

So just who are we supposed to love? To whom do we offer Agape? To all our brothers and sisters. To every color, creed, and race. If we dig deep enough we are more alike than we are different. We need to focus on our similarities instead of our differences. Easier said than done. What about someone who has hurt or betrayed us? Yes. A friend who talks behind our back? Yes. A coworker who takes the credit for our project? Yes. A driver who cuts us off on the freeway? Yes. A relative who betrays us with lies or untoward behavior? Yes.

Lewis B. Smedes, in his amazing book *Forgive and Forget,* wrote something that stuck to me like gum on my shoe:

> *To forgive is to set a prisoner free and discover that the prisoner was you! Forgiving does not erase the bitter past. A healed memory is not a deleted memory. Instead, forgiving what we cannot forget creates a new way to remember. We change the memory of our past into a hope for our future.*

The author goes on to say, *"Forgiving is love's toughest work, and love's biggest risk. When we forgive evil we do not excuse it, we do not tolerate it, we do not smother it. We look the evil full in the face, call it what it is, let its horror shock and stun and enrage us, and only then do we forgive it."*

And there it is. Forgive ... then forget and move on. That is love. Moreover, we need to forgive ourselves as well. Each of us makes the best decisions we can based on our current awareness. But we can have a shift in awareness, in other words, the way we see things. When we change the way we look at things, the things we look at change. In a word, it's *perspective.*

Mother Teresa once said, *"Intense love does not measure, it just gives. What can you do to promote world peace? Go home and love your family."*

When someone asked him for money, my father used to say, *"Charity begins at home."* It was his misinformed way of saying no to giving time or money. I have had to undo the old and misguided childhood tropes I heard as a young boy. Charity and love must go on beyond our home.

My friend Bern says, "Feelings are not facts!" So true. Act as if, and the feelings will follow. Harvard psychologist Jerome Bruner wrote, "It's possible to act your way into a new way of feeling as opposed to trying to feel your way into a new way of acting." Also true. Remember, everyone you meet is struggling with something. They are all looking for appreciation, respect, understanding, and, oh yes, love. John Lennon sang, "All you need is love ..."

The universal maxim states, *What kind of world would this world be, if everyone in it were just like me?* My loving actions speak louder than my words.

When I was a young boy, I used to read the Ann Landers column. I know that sounds strange, but she was so wise. She wrote, *"Love is friendship that has caught fire. It is a quiet understanding, mutual confidence, sharing and forgiving. It is loyalty through good and bad times. It settles for less than perfection and makes allowances for human weaknesses."*

How can we become more loving? What follows are seven strategies of love I have gathered over the years from my mentors:

1. Forgive and forget wrongs committed by all of your enemies, relatives, and friends.
2. Look for and find the similarities in others.
3. Walk a mile in someone else's shoes. Ask yourself, *If I were in that situation, would I do that? Have I done that before?* In a word, *empathy.*
4. Remember we are all doing the best we can based on our current awareness.
5. Give others a second chance and the benefit of the doubt.
6. Write your grievances and resentment in the sand, your blessings in stone.
7. Act as if and the feelings will follow.

Henry van Dyke, Jr. wrote, *"Time is too slow for those who wait, too swift for those who fear, too long for those who grieve, too short for those who rejoice, but for those who love, time is eternity."*

Great advice.

I said to my grandchildren recently, *"I love you more today than I did yesterday; but not as much as tomorrow."* I meant it.

To forgive is divine, to err is human. Love is divine.

Men exist for the sake of one another.
Marcus Aurelius

14

On Helping Others

When I'm old I'll assist the less fortunate and offer a helping hand,
And I'll keep my good works a secret, now won't that be just grand?

"Service above self," William used to say. Who else says that exactly? The people William introduced me to on my journey are not only wildly successful in financial terms (not the only measure by any means) but also possess the most joy and peace of mind. They consistently help others without any consideration of payment or recompense.

When I was in my teens, if someone gave me a gift, no matter how small, it always made me happy. In my twenties I began giving gifts to others. However, in those early days, it was conditional, as I waited for something in return. I soon discovered that I was bartering and this attitude brought me less joy. In my thirties a mentor said to me, quoting Mark Twain, *"You can't give someone flowers without getting some of that good smell on yourself."* As I continued giving my time, attention, and resources to people and causes I believed in, I learned something that has stayed with me all these years: *"I can be happy if someone gives me a gift—but I can be just as happy, if not more, if I give a gift to someone else! So that means there is no limit to the joy I can have in my life if I keep giving with no expectation of anything in return."*

It's called *altruism*. Webster defines it as *"selfless concern for the well-being of others, consideration, self-denial"*

Twelve-Step Programs around the world espouse three things:

1. Trust God
2. Clean House
3. <u>Help Others</u>

You will hear a sober person ask, 'I don't get to keep it unless I give it away?' IT? Why, that is simply a new way of life. A different way to see the world in thoughts, feelings, actions, and philosophy."

William told me a story on a long walk one August day. "The great stoic of the Holocaust, Victor Frankl's bestselling book *Man's Search for Meaning* explored the question of meaning under the most horrible of conditions. A Viennese neurologist and professor following in the footsteps of Sigmund Freud, Frankl survived more than two and a half years in Nazi concentration camps thanks to his life-changing and powerful conclusion, *'Everything can be taken from a man but one thing; the last of the human freedoms—to choose one's attitude in any given set of circumstances, to choose one's own way.'* This idea helped him help others.

"During this time he observed and experienced ghastly stress and trauma, and he found himself transfixed by those prisoners who somehow retained, and even magnified, kindness (sharing food and offering words of encouragement), integrity (keeping their word to themselves and others), dignity amidst the inhumanity. Eventually, he concluded that even in the worst pain, human beings can choose to infuse meaning into suffering by saying, *'What is to give light must endure burning.'* At night he would practice what he called *logotherapy,* that is, visualizing being back in Vienna speaking to students about how he survived the concentration camps. Survive he did."

"So he believed in service over self as a way of being?"

"Indeed," William replied, "in ways few of us could ever endure, understand, or apply."

Pausing to process what William had shared, I interjected, "I met the legendary UCLA basketball coach John Wooden in 1993. It was a life-changing experience. He only spoke for an hour (he was 93 at the time!). He said, *'Be true to yourself, help others, make each day your masterpiece, make friendship a fine art, drink deeply from good books—especially the Bible, build a shelter against a rainy day, give thanks for your blessings, and pray for guidance every day.'*

"Okay, I'm sold on helping others. Where do I start?" I asked William.

Smiling, he replied, "Like any new behavior, in little ways. Help an elderly woman with her bag in the overhead compartment on an airplane, give a child some encouraging words if you see them struggling, open the door for the person behind you. Start small and build from there. Be an empathetic ear to a friend or colleague and really listen actively without judgment or unsolicited advice. Be a sounding board—Just listen, then paraphrase the emotions you hear. When they are done talking, ask, 'So what CAN you do? What is out of your control?' Asking those two questions is at the heart of Stoicism. In my observation and experience, not one person in ten does that habitually. A leader's job is not to do the work for others, it's to help others figure out how to do it themselves, to get things done, and to succeed beyond what they thought possible. In other words, become a servant leader. It's the Book of Luke in action."

As if what he shared wasn't enough, he continued. "One of my comedy heroes is Carol Burnett. She's a fearless comedian. She said, *'It's also selfish because it makes you feel good when you help others. I've been helped by acts of kindness from strangers. That's why we're here, after all, to help others.'* I like to call helping others *"enlightened self-interest."* It's about building connections with others. We need each other."

I hated to interrupt William but I felt the need to interject. "When I first began speaking in public it was to sports teams and high-school kids. I still speak to sports teams: high school and college, but it's usually because a client asks me to for his child's sports team. I do it for free, *pro bono,* Latin for *for the public good.* It's a kind of tithing of my time. It's so fulfilling. You see, I was 14 years old when I attended my first seminar. I heard Bob Moawad speak four times before my senior year of high school. Years later, we shared the stage around the country. He and I had a special connection right up until the day he passed away. He was a generous man. He also tithed his time. Three or four times a year, he would speak for Catholic Charities for the cost of an airline ticket and hotel. I do, too."

"That's called 'The Helpers High,' William said. Pausing for effect, he continued. "That is spot on." He smiled. "A friend of one of my clients called me one day and asked for some advice about writing a book. We talked for an hour. He claims he took 10 pages of notes! Just before we hung up, he asked, 'Can we do this again, it was so valuable. Of course I would pay you!' I was speechless. 'How much should I charge?' I inquired. 'Heck, an hour of your time and a question or two once a month, I'd pay $500!' I replied, 'It's a deal.' I became the 'accidental coach.' It's part of how I invest a portion of my time these days. I have had up to ten coaching clients in any given month. Who knew? All because I said YES to helping others without hesitation.

"Leo Buscaglia said, *'The purpose of life is to help others, and if you can't help them, won't you at least not hurt them? I know that is a platitude, that that is sentimental and can easily be attacked. But loving, caring is simple, and we make it complex. Too often we un-derestimate the power of a touch, a smile, a kind word, a listening ear, an honest compliment, or the smallest act of caring, all of which have the potential to turn a life around.'"*

"So it's service over self?" I said.

"Indeed. How about you? How can you help others? Keep looking for ways to give—to increase your service to others."

Message delivered, message received.

Forward, as occasion offers. Never look round to see whether any shall note it ... Be satisfied with success in even the smallest matter, and think that even such a result is no trifle.

Marcus Aurelius

15

On Letting Go

When I'm Old I will remember what was said to me, you are such a silly sod,
Why not, young man, just let it go and let God?

I met William's best friend Pastor Paul over lunch. William had said, "You two need to meet, you have so much in common!" Whenever there was some aspect of my personal development that needed addressing, William used that line before he introduced me to someone who could help. It worked every time and it was just what was needed at that moment. The people he introduced me to were extraordinary human beings.

At lunch, Pastor Paul said, "Have you ever heard the phrase 'Let go and let God?'"

"No," I said.

He continued, "Prayer is simply talking to God (or whatever higher power you believe in), while meditation, on the other hand, is listening for the answers. Some of my most powerful and long-lasting insights have come to me while waiting for an answer to a poem or prayer. Driving and working out, even showering, that's when my best ideas come. I keep a journal handy to capture them."

It was easy to see why he was so successful. This man could tell a story. I leaned forward so as not to miss a word.

"In my early thirties, for more than ten years, I scoured retail shops, Goodwill stores, thrift shops for inspirational plaques with aphorisms that touched my heart and head. I put them up in the "man cave" bathroom—there must have been over 50 of them. One of them read, *'Only one life that soon is past, only what's done with love will last.'*

"There is something healing about prayer and meditation regardless to whom you pray. I say poetry and commandments (mine and others) are like a prayer. Most people read about 250 words per minute. Poems and prayers are meant to be read slowly, around 100-120 words per minute, savoring every line."

Like William, he could spin a yarn and cite ideas that flowed from him like Mount Vesuvius.

He continued, "Why not you? When you find yourself in a hole, the first thing to do is stop digging. Then?

1. Write down the problem. Describe it in detail.
2. Ask yourself, *What would it mean to me to be on the other side of this?*
3. Pray for ideas and insights.
4. Wait and meditate for 15-20 minutes.
5. Do this every day at the same time each day.
6. Don't concern yourself if answers are slow in coming; be patient.
7. Keep it up until you solve the problem or still feel stuck.
8. If stuck, call a mentor, coach, sponsor, teacher, or boss you respect.
9. Talk it out, ask them to be your sounding board.

10. Take action on the ideas that emerge from them.
11. Journal the progress and write down your WINS and lessons learned.
12. Teach this process to someone else.

"Let go and let God. You'll be glad you did." Pastor Paul sat back and smiled a self-contented smile. I had written five pages of notes in my journal. I turned to the waiter and said, "Please bring me the check." It seemed the least I could do after the spiritual seminar I just attended. William had a grin on his face, like a loving father has when his child understands a message. Mission accomplished.

> *You have power over your mind—not outside events.*
> *Realize this, and you will find strength.*
> Marcus Aurelius

16

On Saying Goodbye

And when I'm old I'll say goodbye, it's been one heck of a ride,
With all of you dear readers, ever at my side.

My German friends say *Auf wiedersehen which* means, *Until we meet again; goodbye for the present.* I like that better than *Later, dude ...*

I woke up early without an alarm today. I glanced at the clock in an unfamiliar room. 05:07. I checked in on my sister. She was holding a vigil, sleeping in the hospital bed brought in just for my mother. "You okay? Need anything?" I asked.

"I didn't sleep much," she replied. "If you want to sit with Mum for a while, I will try to get some sleep."

Pausing for a moment to consider the request, I said, "I'll get some coffee and then spell you." I went out to my truck to get what was left of yesterday's coffee. You see, Coupeville, Washington, though it might be the Mussel Mecca of the United States, is still just a bucolic little burg of 1,800 residents on Whidbey Island without a Starbucks. The coffee shop on the pier isn't open at 0515. I stumbled into the kitchen to reheat my old coffee. As I looked around, I asked myself, *Where's the microwave?* I looked all over the kitchen and dining room. Nothing. Who doesn't have a microwave?

Generational gaps are about differences, not similarities. Age, gender, nationalities, us vs. them. Evidently, my mother never thought she needed a microwave. She was born in 1932. I still remember my first one, a Panasonic. It was the size of a Volkswagen Bug. It was given to us by my in-laws in 1982. We used it every day for 18 years. Do you own a microwave? Of course you do. Why? It's fast and easy. Americans love fast and easy. I grabbed a pan, turned on the gas stove, and heated up yesterday's coffee the old-fashioned way, slow and hard. It took about seven minutes (instead of 60 seconds). I sat on the deck, grabbed the last book my mother was reading, Mitch Albom's *Have a Little Faith.* I began to read and wait. That was a blessing. I caught the sunrise coming up over Puget Sound. It was exactly what I needed. A little time to ponder, some perspective. Slow down. Reflect.

It wasn't quite a year ago we all met "Nanny" for breakfast over the holidays. My little family of five and my mother. We had a grand time. All the boys were in the same time zone and area code. She was in her glory. She has been a huge part in their development. She consistently gave them family history, unconditional love, tender loving care and gentle guidance that only a grandmother can provide.

Grief doesn't have stages. Grief has facets. ***Shock, Denial, Anger, Bargaining, Acceptance.*** As we navigate through those extreme emotions, we jump around, in no particular order, like a pinball in the machine. Emotions are all over the place as we cry, laugh, or get mad. Then we turn to what we know for solace and comfort. My brother plays his guitar, his best friend for 45 years. My sister goes into full-throttle Nurse Helen mode, serving, caring, nurturing. I grab my journal and start to write. It's how I cope. It's how I process the grief. I make lists. It helps.

I remembered William's story about his mother. Now it was my turn. Our mothers shared the same first and middle name. My list turned out to be an echo of his list.

It's a simple little exercise that only takes a few minutes. A quick list, written or verbal. It's a mini celebration. It's a way to honor a loved one. I could only remember five.

Five great things about Barbara Jean Matteson:

1) *She was kind, loving and compassionate—the glue that bound all the diverse personalities in our crazy family together; the voice of reason and objectivity.*

2) *She loved to read, especially books; fiction, non-fiction, always borrowed from the library.*

3) *She was a woman of letters; she wrote them religiously, every day, to her mother and friends, old-school, with pen and paper, envelopes and stamps.*

4) *Her English accent was charming and people enjoyed being around her. She was always very polite, very proper, very British. Always a please and thank you so much.*

5) *She made a mean cup of tea. She had rules about making it. It's why she never had a microwave. There are some things that just aren't done.*

So now you know the answer to the question, *Who doesn't have a microwave?* My mother. Sometimes fast and easy isn't best.

Making the time to heat up a cup of tea in a kettle gives us time to think, to slow down, to enjoy the process. I need to stop writing now. My sister needs me to spell her. It's almost time now, time for Jean to join Robert. He is waiting impatiently. 55 years of marriage will do that. The sweet hereafter ... with no microwaves.

After I finished writing this, my sister said, "The microwave is above the stove. How could you have missed it?" Answer? I'm just a guy ... grappling with the facets of grief. Nanny passed away on June 27th, 2010 at 9:55 p.m. surrounded by her family, with waves of love and prayers. She slipped the surly bonds of Earth to touch the face of God.

This poem by Clare Harner gave me solace:

Do not stand at my grave and weep.
I am not there. I do not sleep.
I am a thousand winds that blow.
I am the diamond glints on snow.
I am the sunlight on ripened grain.
I am the gentle autumn rain.
When you awaken in the morning's hush
I am the swift uplifting rush
Of quiet birds in circled flight.
I am the soft stars that shine at night.
Do not stand at my grave and cry;
I am not there. I did not die.

The act of dying is one of the acts of life.
Marcus Aurelius

17

On Comfort Zones

*When I'm old I'll have courage, the foremost quality you feel
down to the bone, it's really a habit of taking risks and stretching
your comfort zone.*

For the very first time, I sat waiting for William to arrive. I had arrived 30 minutes early to finish reading a book about Winston Churchill that I simply could not put down. William noticed my book and offered up a non sequitur over tea. "Did you know Winston Churchill was half Brit, half Yank? His mum was an American aristocrat from a wealthy family and his father was a famous politician who died when Sir Winston was young. He struggled in school, but contended that flunking English three times was a blessing. He was forced to learn and develop an extraordinary command of the English language."

Without pausing to take a breath, William continued. "When he was 23 years old, in the three years he spent as a young soldier in India, he asked his mum to mail him a trunk filled with his father's books and, as the story goes, while everyone else slept in the suffocating and oppressive heat of the afternoon, he devoured dozens of books that would form the foundation of his writing life."

Smiling, I began to take notes. Not wanting to interrupt this lesson, I said, "Do go on ..."

He did. "Most people don't realize what a prolific writer Sir Winston was. Did you know that, between writing speeches, articles for magazines and newspapers, and his countless books, he put over ten million words on paper? Prodigious doesn't quite describe his output. He was one of my writing mentors."

"That is a staggering amount of writing," I said. "Just how did he make the time between all his other responsibilities?"

"In a way, he was forced to. Members of Parliament didn't make much money back then, not like politicians do in this country. MP's had to find other sources of income—for the other members, they simply came from wealthy families that HAD money. Like Teddy Roosevelt, for additional income he had to supplement his military and political pay with his writing. At 23 years of age, he wrote his first novel while he was in India! Then, as a cub reporter on the front lines in Cuba, he wrote about the Spanish-American War for a London Newspaper. The revenue of 70 years of writing not only paid his bills, along with speaking engagements in America, it made him famous above and beyond his political ambitions and military accomplishments!"

As William shared his insights about someone he considered one the world's greatest leaders, he told me about his visit to the Churchill War Rooms museum in London which offers tourists a glimpse of what it was like in the darkest days of World War II. What follows are insights into Sir Winston's philosophy and quotes:

I'm always willing to learn; but I prefer not to be taught!

The longer you look back, the farther you can look forward ...

Success in any endeavor always demands a greater effort.

His speech to his alma mater, Harrow, in 1941, was short and sweet: *"Never give in, never, never, never, never in nothing great or small, large or petty—never give in except to convictions of honor and good sense!"* Then he sat down. (Each time he said "Never" he pounded his cane on the floor for emphasis!)

We must not lose our faculty to dare, particularly in dark days.

No one should waste a day!

As long as the job is done, it does not matter much who gets the credit.

How little we should worry about anything except doing our best.

Plant a garden in which you can sit when digging days are done.

Only one link in the chain of destiny can be handled at a time.

I get my exercise serving as a pallbearer to my many friends who exercised all their lives!

We are all worms; but I do believe I am a glow worm.

In critical and baffling situations it is always best to recur to first principles and then simple action!

How often in life must one be content with what one can get.

It's easier to break a crockery than to mend it.

When we face with a steady eye the difficulties which lie before us, we may derive new confidence from remembering those we have already overcome!

William's face turned very serious as he continued. "By his extraordinary able example, this great man pushed me out of my comfort zone and I was inspired to write each day and write as well as I could. I used what I like to call my 'Staircase Method.' William drew it in his journal to make his point easy to see and understand.

Audio Book

Book

e-book

Special Reports

Ezine

Magazine Article

"So like a set of stairs, you walk up one step at a time until you have a finished product?" I asked.
"Indeed …"
"With your kind permission, I'm going to borrow that process! It will definitely push me out of my comfort zone."

"By Jove, I think he's got it!" he said with a smirk. I picked up the tab.

A man's worth is no greater than his ambitions.
Marcus Aurelius

18

On Acting Now

But wait just one hot minute, I'm just not that young anymore,
I guess that means I'M OLD RIGHT NOW, as I tally up the score!

Ll we really have is right now. One day at a time. 24 little hours. Yesterday is past, gone. Tomorrow is a promissory note. We have the gift of today. It's why we call it the present. Why do we put things off? Why do we procrastinate on something important? Ben Franklin posited there are two reasons: *"The task is going to take more than 45 minutes and/or the direction of the task is unclear."*

In 1982, Wall of Voodoo, an obscure American rock band out of Los Angeles, came to prominence with a minor hit on alternative radio and MTV called "Tomorrow." I believe it was popular because its lyrics hit close to home for so many people:

Wake up in the morning, pull myself outta bed.
Think about the night before, and everything I said.
I made lots of promises, I know that I can't keep.
So I'll do it tomorrow, that sounds like a pretty good idea to me.

Sometimes, the reason for not acting now can be explained by comfort zones. On a deeper level, it could be fear of criticism.

My sophomore year I attended my first high school dance. I leaned against a wall with my friend Brian, a six-foot-three, 240-pound football player. Waiting for what, I had no clue. For the girls on the other side of the gym to ask *us* to dance? I don't think so. It was a scene right out of *West Side Story*. Brian broke the silence and said, "I'd dance with her!"

"Who?" I asked, like a detective interviewing a perp.

"The blond, blue dress, five-foot-three!"

"Jill?" I replied. "She just moved here from Florida. She is really smart. And nice. She is in my typing class. You should totally ask her to dance."

After a long pause he replied, "Oh, no. Not me!"

"Hey, man, what are you afraid of?"

Silence. At first, I thought it was the obvious answer: rejection.

Thinking about it deeply, I realized I was wrong. What he was really afraid of was *The Long Walk Back* after the potential rejection. Worrying about something that had not yet happened! I made a decision right then and there. I was going to ask every girl against that wall to dance, one at a time. If they all said no, I was going out the side door to get drunk (we had beer stashed in the woods!) The fourth girl said yes and I was dancing up a storm.

Near the end of the basketball game of life, as we enter the fourth quarter, we regret the things we never tried. Regret can be turned into a positive point of view. When we regret a lost opportunity, bad investment, past deed or misstep, we usually say, **"If only ..."** *If only I had finished college; If only I had finished my degree;*

If only I had joined the military; If only I had kept my marriage together—it can be a long list if we let it be. It's kind of self-inflicted mental and emotional torture. Instead, try changing the narrative with a simple phrase: **"At least..."** *At least I went to college for a year and learned how to study and how to create my own curriculum; At least I found a career I love; At least I learned a great deal about how to be a good husband by being a bad one ...*

Turning IF ONLY into AT LEAST will help you use the power of regret to *Learn from the past, Plan for the future, Live for today.* Good advice from Pastor Paul who puts pithy quotes on his church's billboard. He also says, *"When you encourage you get courage!"* I like that.

One of my all-time favorite poets is Ella Wheeler Wilcox. Her poems were inspiring and ahead of her time. She once wrote, *"The man who radiates good cheer, who makes life happier wherever he meets it, is always a man of vision and faith."* My favorite poem of hers is entitled *Will.*

There is no chance, no destiny, no fate,
Can circumvent or hinder or control
The firm resolve of a determined soul.
Gifts count for nothing; will alone is great;
All things give way before it, soon or late.
What obstacle can stay the mighty force
Of the sea-seeking river in its course,
Or cause the ascending orb of day to wait?
Each well-born soul must win what it deserves.
Let the fool prate of luck. The fortunate
Is he whose earnest purpose never swerves,
Whose slightest action or inaction serves
The one great aim. Why, even Death stands still,
And waits an hour sometimes for such a will.

Today is the day for action. Time waits for no man or woman. As the folks from Nike said so simply, "Just Do It!" No regrets.

Be content with what you are, and wish not change;
nor dread your last day, nor long for it.
Marcus Aurelius

19

On Leaving It All on the Ice

When I'm old I'll be a good sport and strive to be nice,
Like the hockey players of old, leave it all on the ice?

Would you say you are a competitive person? Do you hate to lose or do you love to win?

I am one of the most competitive guys I know. Basketball, cribbage, sales, pick a game. I want to win. I hate losing. In fact, I hate losing more than I love to win. It's hardwired into my DNA. I got it from my old man. I look for every advantage, every edge to win. In high school I got into fights on the hardwood—perhaps that is an exaggeration—it was mostly just shoving and name-calling. I talked trash. I'm not proud of that. My boys played basketball at the highest levels in high school, college, and overseas professionally. I never did that. I married well. I'm just saying ...

Our youngest son, Evan, was a promising young hockey player at 10 years of age. He was fearless. He skated with reckless abandon and always played tough defense. A problem arose one day when he had a baseball game, a basketball game, and a hockey game, ALL IN ONE DAY. We were up at 0400 that morning for hockey and didn't get home until late that night.

The next day, I sat him down and said, "Son, you are such a great athlete. I love watching you play all three sports but it's just too much. You have to pick two." He dropped hockey. It was probably just as well. You don't see too many six-foot-eleven guys in the NHL.

Unless you are a lifelong hockey fanatic and/or a student of sports history, you've probably never heard the following story. William shared it with me one day over tea.

"When professional hockey was in its infancy, there were six original teams. They played each other 15 times in a season. Real hatred sprang up. Real teeth got knocked out. Real eyes were gouged. By the end of the season, these guys wanted to kill each other. Yet, despite this negative dynamic, a custom took hold in the 1930's. After each game, the players lined up on the ice and shook hands, consoling each other. They still do today. The NBA adopted this custom as well. Unique in sports."

When the game is over, no matter how heated things get, we all need to show appreciation, respect, and understanding. During challenging times, for whatever reason, we look to professional sports to give us cues to show us the way. What if civility, empathy, compassion, kindness were the order of the day in sports and life?

John Cena, the actor and wrestler, said, *"Be loyal to those who are loyal to you. And respect everyone, even your enemies and competition."*

Simone Biles, the gold-medal gymnast, said, *"A successful competition for me is always going out there and putting 100 percent into whatever I'm doing. It's not always winning. People, I think, mistake that it's just winning. Sometimes it could be, but for me, it's hitting the best sets I can, gaining confidence, and having a good time and having fun."*

Iconic 1970's sports reporter Howard Cosell, said, *"The ultimate victory in competition is derived from the inner satisfaction of knowing that you have done your best and that you have gotten the most out of what you had to give."*

We need to take a page from hockey players of yore. Compete like crazy, do the very best you can, give it 100%, and leave it all on the ice.

My late friend Ron Haight was a serious hockey player. He used to say, "I went to a fight and a hockey game broke out!" I love that.

Life is too short for resentment, hatred, animus, hard feelings, and ill will.

Why not form a new custom? After a heated game, in whatever game you play, why not line up, shake your opponents' hands, give the half-hug, dap, or high five?

When the game's over, I leave it on the ice. How about you?

PS: Last Christmas I gave our son Evan a cribbage board to honor his time in college as an All-American basketball player. (He was drafted into the D-League and ended up playing professionally overseas in Norway and Japan.) I played him in Cribbage the other day on HIS board, on HIS home court. He skunked me. I STILL hate to lose ...

Kindness is unconquerable, so long as it is without flattery or hypocrisy. For what can the most insolent man do to you, if you contrive to be kind to him, and if you have the chance gently advise and calmly show him what is right ... and point this out tactfully and from a universal perspective. But you must not do this with sarcasm or reproach, but lovingly and without anger in your soul.

Marcus Aurelius

20

On Looking Forward

When I'm old I'll work on my goals and they will go to work on me,
As the process manifests for the whole wide world to see.

It was clear to me that William was slowing down. He still had that sparkle in his eyes and passion for teaching, but the words came slower, with longer pauses. He smiled and began. "I remember when the Beatles came to Shea Stadium in New York in 1965. The country was in mourning over John F. Kennedy's death and it was as if the Beatles were ordered up by God to give us all a reason for hope, singing along with their positive message and inspiring love songs. It's been said a hit song has two qualities: It's personal and it's universal, touching us on a personal level for our own reasons and universal like falling in love or heartbreak. With John, Paul, George, and Ringo it was truly a magical mystery tour. John Lennon was the leader and after the Beatles broke up he recorded the song 'Imagine.'

> *Imagine all the people*
> *Living life in peace ...*

"Most people do not use their imagination in the right way. Worry, fear, uncertainty, and doubt are negative forms of imagination. Job 3:25 says, *'For the thing which I greatly **fear** comes upon me ...'* However, we have a choice. The wisdom of centuries is packed into laconic advice. The essence of Stoicism, perhaps the most durable and useful school of thought ever devised, comes from second-century Roman emperor Marcus Aurelius. The Stoics taught that life well lived requires deep understanding of what we CAN control, and—more difficult—all that lies beyond our control. We determine nothing but our own actions and reactions, our willful reasoned choices.

"At the risk of repeating myself, this analogy begs to be retold. Teddy Roosevelt understood how to use imagination; moreover, he knew how to inspire others to as well. In July of 1898 in the San Juan Heights, Cuba, prior to the last big assault up Kettle Hill to win the war, Colonel Roosevelt walked around camp encouraging his men and asking them a simple question: 'What are you looking forward to AFTER the war?' Then he would listen and reply 'Bully!' and move on to the next man. He understood the power of imagination, the efficacy of having something meaningful to look forward to.

"It's vital to understand the difference between the brain and the mind. The brain is a computer, the mind is the software, the *apps* if you will. Learning how use and apply the mind is the strangest secret in the world."

I was grateful that I had the foresight to bring my journal and a pen. I began to scribble what would end up being the last key words from my mentor, teacher, coach, and dear friend. He delivered his longest sermon and perhaps the most important one ...

104

"In 1957 Alex F. Osborne, a brilliant researcher and writer, wrote a book that changed my life entitled *Applied Imagination*. He broke down how the mind works in relation to the various uses of imagination and a positive use of visualization.

1) **Speculative imagery**
2) **Reproductive imagery**
3) **Structural imagery**
4) **Creative expectancy**
5) **Creative action**

"**Speculative imagery.** You may never have visited Niagara Falls but you can recall a picture you have seen. Simply recline on your bed, look at the ceiling, and make yourself SEE the extraordinary cataract in all its glory. In a word, it's fantasy.

"**Reproductive imagery.** In this second aspect, imagination is concerned with the past. It's going back in your past and recalling a success, a proud WIN, a positive accomplishment, like rewinding a video to watch a scene over and over again. The key is to only use this form with POSITIVE experiences, never the negative ones. Rewinding to recall a confident moment so you can fast forward using past success to fuel future results is using your successful past to deliberately bring pictures back into your mind and willfully direct these photographic powers.

"**Structural imagery.** Structural visualization is the third phase of imagery. Pilots use flight simulators to train young pilots. We can use the same principle to improve our skills and manifest desired outcomes. It's using a blueprint to foster specific results. The process is simple. Find someplace quiet, turn off all the devices, sit, breathe deeply, relax, go back in your mind's eye, and remember a past WIN. Hold it for a moment, remember the positive emotion associated with the memory, then fast forward to the future outcome you seek in all its glorious future detail, as if it were happening now. Like pilots taking off or landing a plane, simulate the desired outcome in detail and with positive emotion. Simple. Do it several times a day, morning, noon, and night. Do it for 21-35 days and it will become a habit. Your brain stores the imagined event as real in your subconscious, for future use.

"**Creative expectancy.** The highest form of anticipative imagination is creative expectancy. When we look forward to something we want to come true, and strongly believe that it *will* come true, we can more often than not make it come true through repetition, emotion, and time. Babe Ruth understood this attitude. One day, during a doubleheader, he struck out eight times. A reporter asked him, 'Babe, are you worried?' Smiling, the Bambino replied, 'You have to understand, I hit a home run once in every eleven at bats. I would not want to be pitching against me tomorrow. I'm DUE!' The next game he hit two home runs and the Yankees won the pennant again. That is positive creative expectancy in action.

"**Creative action.** When you begin to affirm aloud your goals (better still, write them in a journal) on a daily basis, and you are crystal clear on your WHAT and WHY, the HOW begins to assemble, like a jigsaw puzzle coming together. Your reticular activating system, or RAS, is a series of web-shaped fibers about the size of a walnut in the back of your brain. It's your personal GPS. It opens up your senses and finds the ideas, books, people, systems, information needed to accomplish your goals. When the ideas appear, and they will if you are faithful to the process, write them down and take action. Some people call it the Holy Spirit, others Universal Intelligence. Whatever it is, it works, if you have faith in the process and persist. Trust the process. It will change your life as it has changed mine.

"You see, the word APPLIED is what matters. The key word is *action.* Imagination means nothing without application. Look forward, foresee, supply, complete, plan, invent, solve, advance, originate. Note there is not a single passive verb in this list.

"The mind is like a thermostat. It regulates our comfort zones. It creates our self-image which is composed of historical evidence of our abilities. The more hard things you push yourself to do, the more competent you will see yourself to be.

"Have you ever played nine holes of golf and shot a 35? Your buddy says, 'Wow, you had 35 on the front nine! Nice going!' Because you are a 15 handicap, your self-image adjusts for the error and you shoot a 52 on the back nine. Why? You see yourself as shooting 87 consistently. It is a handicap and fixed setting on your golf thermostat. Change the setting and change the score and how you see yourself on the links."

I interrupted William with a story of my own, as if to echo and affirm his insights. He smiled and leaned back in his chair to sip his tea and listen. "My senior year of basketball, in the biggest game of the year against our archrival, I went 0-9 in the first half. I was on the bench at halftime, feeling sorry for myself. The JV coach, Earl Wayman, saw me in the middle of my pity party and sat next to me. 'Why are you sitting here and not warming up?' I looked up and said, 'Coach, I missed every shot I took in the first half!' He smiled and said, 'Let me ask you a question. What do you shoot from the field, you know, your field goal percentage?' I replied, '54%, why?' He said, 'Well as far as I can tell, you got ALL your misses out of the way! We need you in the second half if we are going to win. Stop feeling sorry for yourself.' I jumped up and began to warm up. I went 9-9 in the second half, 18 points. We set a school record for points in a game and locked up first place."

William was silent, letting me process my own story, allowing me to understand and appreciate it all.

"So I need to adjust my personal thermostat and have faith it will do its job in every area of my life, financial, fitness, interpersonal, spiritual."

"Exactly, my young friend. Indeed!"

The last time I saw William we were having breakfast at his favorite diner. It was the last story I would tell him. He just sat back and listened. The student was about to become the teacher.

"In my eighth-grade year, I turned out for basketball. I had played one season of hoops the year before on the suggestion of my Little League Baseball coach, Gus Cooper. It was a decision that would alter my life forever. After two days of tryouts, the roster was posted, and my name wasn't on it. It was a rite of passage, a defining moment. When you get hit with that kind of adversity at such a tender age, one of two things happens: You shrink or you grow. I got mad. I was on a mission to prove coach Kim Wilson wrong. I would show him.

"Webster defines a GOAL as *the object of a person's ambition or effort; an aim or desired result. Objective, end, target, intention, aspiration, dream, desire.* The following week, I approached the best player I knew, Kenny Christensen. He was an eighth-grader on the ninth-grade team scoring 20 points per game. He had more moves than a can of worms. His shot was picture-perfect. He had supreme confidence on and off the court. In short, he had what I wanted. Even though we were the same age, he was a mentor. I asked him, 'How did you get so good at basketball?' He looked me right in the eye and said, 'No one has ever asked me that before!' Smiling, he continued, 'I shoot two hours a day and I attend Bob Houbreg's basketball camp in the summer.' The next day he brought me a brochure. *Camp Casey, July. $110.* I informed my parents I was going to this camp. My father smiled and said, 'You earn half, I'll pay the other half.' He saw the gleam in my eye, the fire in my belly. The following weekend, he nailed a hoop to the shed and gave me an old leather basketball and said, 'Show me how hard you are willing to work.' I wore out the grass and the net over the next six months. I shot in the rain and snow, two hours a day. The next summer he called a friend and they built a proper concrete court and ten-foot hoop. I continued to shoot two hours every day without fail, with game-like intensity. That summer I attended camp. I received instruction on how to practice, valuable game experience, and inspiration.

"The following year my name was on the roster. #12. Goal achieved.

"I attended two weeks of camp the next year. The following summer I refereed games to pay for my three weeks of camp. By my junior year, I was the starting center (at age 15) on the varsity. Letters from colleges arrived like snowflakes from the sky. I have been setting goals ever since.

"As I reflect upon that time, analyzing what I did OFF the court, some insights bubble to the surface. In hindsight, basketball had become my "Magnificent Obsession," much like speaking and writing is now. What else did I do besides practice two hours a day?

1) I read every book on basketball I could find.

2) I devoured the sports page every day and read magazine articles in *Sporting News* and *Sports Illustrated,* looking for ideas and insights to propel me forward.

3) I found open gyms five nights a week and played like my life depended upon it.

4) I played UP against older kids every chance I could. I found mentors and models.

5) I watched what little basketball was on TV. In the *College Game of the Week* one Saturday in 1967, I saw "Pistol" Pete Maravich, the LSU shooting guard, score 68 points and 12 assists.

6) I attended every high-school and college game I could, studying the best players of the time.

7) I made friends with the janitor and secured keys to the gym and lights.

8) I shot AFTER practice, sometimes until 10:00 p.m., five nights a week.

9) I wrote goals specific to basketball in every category—points, rebounds, free-throw percentages, etc.—onto 3x5 cards and affirmed them five times a day with positive emotion.

10) I VISUALIZED the perfect game over and over again until, one day, it happened.

"No one had to tell me to do all these things; it was a 'WANT to' not a 'HAVE to.' With each passing season, my **K.A.S.H.** improved: **K**nowledge, **A**ttitude, **S**kills, **H**abits. I was a sponge. I lived and slept basketball."

William, having waited patiently, said, "That is a pitch-perfect example of Osborn's philosophy. Thomas Jefferson said, '*Nothing can stop the man with the right mental attitude from achieving his goal; nothing on earth can help the man with the wrong mental attitude. Obstacles are those frightful things you see when you take your eyes off your goal.*'

"Vince Lombardi said, '*Leaders aren't born they are made. And they are made just like anything else, through hard work. And that's the price we'll have to pay to achieve that goal, or any goal.*'

"What is your number-one goal? Why do you want it? How much? By When? The right kinds of goals do not include the HOW. Forget the HOW. Trust the process. The how will come if you affirm your number-one goal long enough. Affirm with passion and positive emotion over and over again. Have faith. Persist."

When William was through affirming my insights, I continued. "Remembering my success with basketball, right around my fifth year as a speaker, my wife asked me why I wasn't doing keynotes and seminars in Hawaii or Arizona? I shrugged and replied, 'Beats me. What's wrong with New York, Boston, Philadelphia, and Minneapolis in January?' 'Just wondering,' she said. The next day, I wrote in my journal, *Find seminars in Hawaii and Arizona, for my wife!* and put a heart around it. Three weeks later, the sales manager for a large HVAC contractor bought my book at the break and asked if I would be willing to come to Honolulu to speak to his team. I replied, 'Let me check with my wife, I'll get back to you!' (I think her response was, 'Giddy-Up!') I have since been to Hawaii nine times and Arizona fifteen times. Simple, isn't it? I did the same thing with Australia."

What do you want to HAVE? DO? SEE? BECOME? SHARE?

Goals will add years to your life and life to your years. The Old Testament says, *Without a Vision, the people perish.* It really is true. *First you work on goals, then they work on you!*, Napoleon Hill wrote in 1935. *A goal is a dream with a deadline.*

What are you looking forward to? Imagine ...

I need to find and thank Coach Kim Wilson. He gave me a great gift by cutting me that November day. My life has never been the same.

William added, "Why not you? What is your number-one goal? What is your definite chief aim and purpose in business? Why not describe the who, what, where, when, how and why?"

Little did I know, this process of goal achievement would transform my life in every way, spiritual, emotional, financial, physical, interpersonal.

Thank you, William Ian Oldham!

You have power over your mind–not outside events.
Realize this, and you will find strength.
Marcus Aurelius

21

On Exercise

When I'm old I will exercise, lift, swim, walk, and run,
It turns out it's good for you and can be great fun!

When someone would ask William how he was, he always said things like, *Good as gold, Right as rain, Fit as a fiddle,* and *Sound as a pound* with great enthusiasm and sincerity. When I asked him one day why he always replied with one of those dated yet pithy British replies, he smiled and said, "I wondered when you were going to ask me because to the untrained ear it sounds a bit cliché, even somewhat arrogant. I say those four responses for *me.* They remind me of what I want to affirm in my life. Is a bird happy because he sings or does he sing because he is happy? Birds sing. Eagles soar. Words matter; they trigger emotions that impact our behavior."

I leaned in to capture every word. I knew what was coming. A stupendous sermon on wellness.

"Let's take *fit as a fiddle.* I wasn't always fit. In point of fact, in my mid-forties, one could say I was fat, obese, even pear-shaped. Middle age is when your broad mind and narrow waist can trade places. That is exactly what happened to me, or rather, what I created."

William was sharing a very personal insight. Not one I suspected he had shared with too many people. He continued, "I had stopped exercising because of an extraordinary demand on my time. For ten years I did over 100 keynotes and traveled 300 days a year. I was eating in the finest restaurants and never saying no to appetizers on the front end and dessert on the back. Walking through airports was my only exercise, and I usually took the elevator or moving sidewalks. I gained five pounds a year for ten years.

"I had just completed a team-building session for the senior team at T-Mobile in Denver. I went to my room, put on my swim trunks, and hopped in the pool. I swam a few laps and stopped, winded. There was a scale in the weight room. I stepped on it. *305 pounds!* Mind you, in college I was a svelte 225. I experienced a moment of clarity. I call it *inspirational dissatisfaction.* I was sick and tired of being sick and tired. That day I made a decision. I would lose 60 pounds or 12 inches off my waist, whichever came first."

"What came next?" I asked.

"Well, you know my approach to any new goal by now. I read ten books on fitness and wellness. Do you remember Jack LaLanne from the sixties?"

"Vaguely. My mother used to watch him on TV. Didn't he sell juicers?"

"Yes, that is the fellow. The juicer he sold on his infomercials was when he was in his eighties and nineties. To understand Jack, you have to know his origin story. It's a dandy.

"He described himself as being a sugarholic and a junk-food junkie until he was 15. He also had behavioral problems, but turned his life around after hearing a lecture about the benefits of good nutrition. During his career, he came to believe that the country's overall health depended on the health of its population, and referred to physical culture and nutrition as 'the salvation of America.'"

"He found a cause and created a movement?" I said.

"Indeed! LaLanne hosted *The Jack LaLanne Show* from 1951 to 1985, he published books on fitness, and preached the health benefits of regular exercise and a good diet.

"He opened America's first modern health club in Oakland, California. He invented a number of exercise machines and popularized juicing and the jumping jack. He produced a series of videos so viewers could be coached virtually. He coached the elderly and disabled to enhance their strength and health."

"Do go on," I said.

"At age 70 he towed 70 boats, carrying a total of 70 people, a mile and a half through Long Beach Harbor."

"What?"

"There's more. Steve Reeves credited LaLanne as his inspiration to build his muscular physique while keeping a slim waist. Arnold Schwarzenegger, as governor of California, placed him on his Governor's Council on Physical Fitness, and on the occasion of LaLanne's death he credited LaLanne for being 'an apostle for fitness' by inspiring billions across the world to live healthier lives."

"So he became a serious mentor to you?" I said.

"Indeed. I bought his book, devoured it, and followed his advice on exercise and nutrition. In 90 days I lost the 60 pounds and 12 inches from my waist. Moreover, I kept it off."

"You are getting so skinny it hurts to sit down?" I replied with a sarcastic tone.

"Fit, not fat. Lean and strong. I incorporated yoga, swimming and speed walking into my weight-lifting routines. I worked out every day but Sunday."

"Do you still have the book by Mr. LaLane?" I asked, secretly hoping he would loan me his copy. I knew William highlighted, annotated, and dog-eared every non-fiction book he read.

"I will give you a copy. I have several."

My copy arrived in the mail two days later. I devoured it. Here are a few of the fitness feats that LaLanne accomplished:

- He swam from Alcatraz to Fisherman's Wharf in San Francisco while handcuffed.
- At age 42, he set the world record for pushups by doing over 1,000 in 23 minutes.
- At age 45, he did 1,000 jumping jacks and 1,000 pull-ups in 1 hour and 22 minutes.
- At age 60, he swam from Alcatraz to Fisherman's Wharf for the second time. This time he not only wore handcuffs, but also towed a 1,000-pound boat.
- LaLanne was in such remarkable shape that he could do one-armed fingertip pushups while in a completely stretched out position!

Jack LaLane lived to be 96 years young. His wife said his favorite expression was "I don't want to *be old*—when I'm old!" Amen.

Inspired by my mentor, over the next ninety days I lost 50 pounds and ten inches off my waist. And, like William, I kept it off.

The object of life is not to be on the side of the majority,
but to escape finding oneself in the ranks of the insane.
Marcus Aurelius

22

On Doing Your Level Best

When I'm old I'll vow in all things to do my level best,
And write as well as I can each day and forget all the rest.

The very last time I met with William, he wanted to meet at The British Pantry for lunch. Despite arriving fifteen minutes earlier than our agreed-upon time, William was already there, reading *The Old Man and the Sea,* Ernest Hemingway's most successful novel.

"Have you ever read this little story by Mr. Hemingway?" he asked with a smile.

"No," I said. "I was supposed to but instead I read the CliffsNotes borrowed from a buddy of mine. I know the gist of it."

William paused for a moment to find just the right words. "Indeed. You need to make me a promise—never do that again. The gist? You missed out on some of the finest writing in literary history. How much do you know about this great writer?"

"He liked to fish and drink a lot. Sorry—that's so lame," I said.

William frowned. "It's more than lame, it's sad. Let's change that, shall we? Take my copy and promise me you will read it in one sitting. It's only 126 pages."

"It's a deal," I said with all the sincerity I could muster.

"Why that's just grand," he said.

I was to learn that Hemingway was born in Oak Park, Illinois in 1899. He began his writing career for *The Kansas City Star* in 1917. During the First World War he volunteered as an ambulance driver on the Italian Front and was seriously wounded. In 1921 he settled in Paris where he became part of the expatriate circle of young writers: Gertrude Stein, F. Scott Fitzgerald, Ezra Pound, and Ford Madox Ford—a kind of mastermind group of great writers. With the appearance of *The Sun Also Rises* he became not only the voice of the "lost generation" but the preeminent writer of his time. In the 1930's he settled in Cuba where he conducted his research on this amazing novella about the old man and the big fish.

William shared what he had learned about Mr. Hemingway—I reached for my journal. He was talking with such passion and detail I knew it was worth capturing as much as I could.

"Do you understand the word *process* as it pertains to writing?" William asked.

"I think so," I replied.

He continued. "As the legend goes, he arose early each day, made a big pot of strong black coffee, grabbed a few yellow legal pads, ten no. 2 pencils sharpened to a fine point, and five Cuban cigars. He wrote until the pencils were dull, the cigars were smoked, and the coffee drunk. He was done writing for the day. He had a 3x5 card on his desk that said, ***"Write as well as you can each day and finish what you start!"***

"At night he would go into town and talk to the locals, fishermen, dock workers, carpenters, blacksmiths. He preferred the company of average workingmen for one simple reason—to listen to the words they used, how they told stories of the sea. He was paying strict attention to how they spoke (dialogue), what they looked like and what they wore (description). His ability to capture the zeitgeist of the time and region made his writing authentic and personal to his readers. THAT was his process."

"So he lived the things he wrote about in both the first and third person?"

"Indeed," William said. "When you read this amazing story, you will understand the phrase "Caught between the devil and the deep blue sea." Continuing, he said, "His tough, terse prose and short declarative sentences did more to change the style of written English than any other writer in the twentieth century. *For Whom the Bell Tolls* is considered his true literary masterpiece. But let's start you off with the story of the big fish."

When we finished our high tea, scones with clotted cream and strawberry jam, William gave me a big hug and held it for longer than I could ever remember. He said, "I'm proud of you. You have come a long way from when first we met. Keep it going. You are on the right track. I love you."

"Thank you, William. You have changed my life in ways I cannot even measure. But why me?"

"Someday ..." was all he said.

We said goodbye for the last time. As William walked away, I had a sad feeling this was the last cup of tea we would share. He passed away a week later.

Accept the things to which fate binds you, and love the people with whom fate brings you together, but do so with all your heart.
Marcus Aurelius

23

The Last Letter

Two weeks to the day after William passed away, a certified letter arrived in the mail.

My Dearest Mark,

I was going through my father's journal dated July 4, 1947. I found a passage I'm not certain I had ever read before. Perhaps I had but it was buried deep in my subconscious. In my father's hand, it read:

William,

I don't believe I ever told you about my best friend in the war. He was a British soldier from just outside of London. One fateful day we were trapped, pinned down by German gunfire. Then, without warning, it stopped. We held our breath in the silence, as the quiet is never a good sign in war. It was only 15-20 minutes, but it felt like fifteen hours. Then, before we had a chance to catch our breath, we saw the enemy charging down the hill with their bayonets, hell-bent for their intended purpose. The biggest guy I ever saw was coming at me at a dead run. My best friend pushed me out of the way and saved my life. He took the bayonet that was intended for me. I shot my enemy dead, the only life I ever took. It haunts me to this day. Not ten minutes later, our reinforcements showed up and dispatched that German infantry in less than 30 minutes. I held my best mate in my arms as he asked me a favor, to look after his family after he was gone. Then his life slipped away as he shuffled off this mortal coil to a better place to touch the hand of God.

Ronald A. Robinson from Hillingdon saved my life that day at the expense of his own. He was the bravest man I ever knew. You see, he was the same Ronald who married your grandmother. The same Ronald who gave me his copy of Meditations *by Marcus Aurelius. Now you know why I memorized that book and his philosophy of life. Now you know why from our very first cup of tea, I felt a spiritual connection with you like no other young student I have ever taught. We are bound by history and blood.*

Remember, the days are long, but the years are short. Tempus fugit. My sincere hope is that you continue to carry the message our forefathers gave their lives for. Don't lose faith. Promise yourself that you will be a success story—and I promise you that all the forces of the universe will unite to come to your aid; you might not feel it today or even for a while, but the longer you wait, the bigger the prize. Our lives are shaped not as much by our experiences as by our expectations. Expect the best. I'll be watching.

May the road rise up to meet you. May the wind be always at your back. May the sun shine warm upon your face; the rains fall soft upon your fields and until we meet again, may God hold you in the palm of His hand.

W.I.O.

Ronald A. Robinson

My maternal grandfather,
killed in action in 1942 and posthumously
awarded The Victoria Cross for bravery.

Epílogue

I grieved the loss of my mentor for a long time. Over the next year, I thought about all the lessons he taught me—the poems and quotes he shared with me. One night, I said a prayer of thanks for having known this great man. As I sat in silence a poem came to me and I wrote it in my journal. Like a puzzle, the verses that began each chapter of his story now come together in a finished poem. This is my tribute to Sir William—Submitted for your approval ...

When I'm Old
by William Ian Oldham

The days go by so fast now, as I turn the calendar pages,
Another year behind me, as my face slowly ages.

Getting old is not for wimps, I heard my father say,
Yet I'm as old as he once was, that time is today.

But when I'm old, much older than this day,
I'll keep my griping to myself, complaining doesn't pay.

When I'm old I'll tell my tales, with all the gratitude I can muster,
And in keeping with Teddy Roosevelt, that famous Trust Buster.

When I'm old I'll seek to inspire and lead by example,
And share the hard-won lessons of my past, perhaps just a sample.

When I'm old I'll laugh at myself and follow Rule 62,
Because I always feel better, every time that I do.

When I'm old I'll practice kindness, of the radical variety,
Then, like Mr. Fred Rogers, I can positively impact society.

When I'm old I'll actively listen more, to everyone I meet,
From the butcher, baker, and candlestick maker and the CEO on Wall Street.

When I'm old I'll exercise my right to walk away,
From the cynics and the whiners, before they wreck my day.

When I'm old I'll make people laugh and tickle their funny bone,
So that their heart's made lighter and they will never feel alone.

When I'm old I'll write those letters, to the teachers who believed in me,
So that they'll know they made a difference in all I do and see.

When I'm old I'll read the Bible and the 100 Greatest Books,
Alone on my deck with a cup of tea, ignoring the dirty looks.

When I'm old I'll say "I love you" to every friend and foe,
Because life is so short, it must be said before I go.

When I'm old I'll assist the less fortunate and offer a helping hand,
And I'll keep my good works a secret, now won't that be just grand?

When I'm old my teacher will say to me, you are such a silly sod,
Why not, my young friend, just let it go and let God?

And when I'm old I'll say goodbye, it's been one heck of a ride,
With all of you dear readers, ever at my side.

When I'm old I'll have courage, the foremost qualities that you feel
down to the bone, it's really a habit of taking risks and stretching
your comfort zone.

But wait just one hot minute, I'm just not that young anymore,
I guess that means I'M OLD RIGHT NOW, as I tally up the score!

So I won't wait to do all these noble deeds, creating love from hate,
I'll do them all from this day forward, before it's all too late.

When I'm old I'll be a good sport and strive to be nice,
Like the hockey players of old, leave it all on the ice?

When I'm old I'll work on my goals and they will go to work on me,
As the process manifests for the whole wide world to see.

When I'm old I will exercise, lift, swim, walk, and run,
It turns out it's good for you and can be great fun!

When I'm old I'll vow in all things to do my level best,
And write as well as I can each day and forget all the rest.

When I'm old ...

A year later, on the anniversary of William's death, his grandson, W.I.O. the 3rd, walked into my office and introduced himself. "You knew my grandfather," is all he said.
"I did, I'll make some tea ..."

127

Acknowledgments

Webster defines *acknowledgment* as an author's or publisher's statement of <u>indebtedness</u> to others, typically one printed at the beginning of a book. I'm choosing to end with the recognition these amazing people gave me; and for all the praise, credit, gratitude, appreciation, hailing, saluting, thank you from the bottom of my heart.

To all the Williams and Wilmas in my long life, from the bottom of my heart, much obliged for all the wisdom and guidance I received on my journey. I can never repay your kindness and affection. There is no such thing as a self-made man. Each of us owes a debt of gratitude to all the coaches, teachers, parents, uncles, aunts, grandparents, friends, mentors, and children who offered helping hands, legs up, kind words, blueprints or able examples.

In chronological order, my heartfelt acknowledgment to:

Yosh-ko-san, my Japanese nanny from age two to six.

Ms. Temple, my second-grade teacher, for the discipline.

Mr. Hopkins, my fourth-grade teacher, for affirming I was funny and smart.

Mrs. Dosser, my seventh-grade teacher, for asking me to speak in front the class about Japan.

Coach Wilson, my eighth-grade basketball coach, who cut me from the team so I could prove him wrong a year later!

Shop teacher Bob Stalder who gave me my first and only A+, in mechanical drawing, for doing 23 extra-credit drawings over Christmas break.

Coach Mosely, my ninth-grade basketball coach, who put me on the roster.

Coach Bruce Evans, my tenth-grade basketball coach, who believed in me.

Coach Earl Wayman, my eleventh-grade coach, who wouldn't let me feel sorry for myself and challenged me to work on getting better.

Mr. Simonson, typing teacher, who took the time to listen to me after class.

Fräulein Susan Hall, German teacher and mentor, who asked me to speak in public for the first time at 23 years of age to some high-school kids.

My Uncle Brian who was a master storyteller with perfect posture and an able example of sartorial splendor.

Auntie Laura, my mum's aunt, who loved me unconditionally and always laughed when I tried to be funny.

Me mum, for inspiring me to write.

My dad, for giving me my first basketball and hoop.

Karl Lechner, service manager, and my first great boss.

Greg Romanoff, my first sales manager, who always encouraged me to grow, learn, and become a speaker.

Bob Moawad, who taught me to set challenging goals, showed me the way in the speaking business, and believed in me.

Charlie "T." Jones, who became my publisher and helped me launch my speaking business. We did three books together before he passed.

Les Dicks, my sales and spiritual mentor.

My three sons, Colin, Evan and Larod, who taught me you can be a really great basketball player, make your teammates better, play great defense, score when your team needs it to win the game, lead your team in every way, defeat your opponents and not be a jerk in the process. In a word, class acts on and off the floor.

Other mentors for their books and examples:
Teddy Roosevelt, Dale Carnegie, Dan Poynter, Winston Churchill, Jim Rohn, Zig Ziglar, Earl Nightingale, Vince Lombardi, John Wooden, Lou Tice.

And to all the clients who hired and rehired me to speak. You know who you are. From the bottom of my heart ... thank you for your trust.

About Mark Matteson

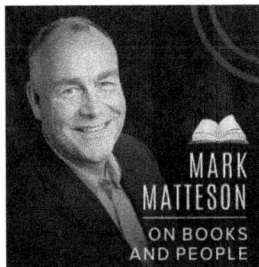

Mark Matteson is an international speaker and the author of the bestselling book *Freedom from Fear* which has sold over 200,000 copies worldwide. He has written six books and ten eBooks. He is one of those rare professionals who can say he is a speaker, consultant, podcaster, publisher, and author and *mean* it. He has attracted clients like Amazon, Microsoft, Honda, Fujitsu, Daikin, Mitsubishi, T-Mobile, John Deere, Conoco-Phillips, Aflac, Honeywell, and other Fortune-100 companies on three continents. He has been called "an edu-tainer," "an oracle of optimism," "a superlative street scholar," and "an intense idea-reporter." Mark travels 250 days a year around the globe, delivering seventy-five keynotes, seminars, and workshops a year. He is a gifted storyteller, using self-effacing humor, high levels of interaction, and powerful and proven business principles to inspire audiences to the highest levels of productivity and profit. Mark leaves audiences wanting more.

Mark began his career in HVAC in 1976. He has been married to Debbie for 44 years and has three grown sons and five grandchildren.

Mark takes great pride in the fact that he once flunked high scool English!

Mark Matteson
Bestselling Author, International Speaker

To order one of my books, go to
www.SparkingSuccess.net/store

Phone: 206.697.0454

To subscribe to Mark's monthly ezine, go to
Mark@SparkingSuccess.net

To watch a few short videos,
visit https://tinyurl.com/8e7udabj

To Listen to my Podcasts, visit:

Google Play: https://tinyurl.com/5n5b5ydn

Apple: https://tinyurl.com/4zvvyy

See Mark Matteson on CEO Zones' *Meet the Speaker* **series!**

"Make it a great day . . . unless you have other plans!"

www.ingramcontent.com/pod-product-compliance
Lightning Source LLC
Chambersburg PA
CBHW070813100426
42742CB00012B/2344